HAGAKURE: BOOK OF THE SAMURAI

by Yamamoto Tsunetomo

Copyright © 2015 by Aloha Library

No part of this book may be reproduced in any written, electronic, recording, or photocopying without written permission of the publisher or author. The exception would be in the case of brief quotations embodied in the critical articles or reviews and pages where permission is specifically granted by the publisher or author.

Although every precaution has been taken to verify the accuracy of the information contained herein, the publisher assume no responsibility for any errors or omissions. No liability is assumed for damages that may result from the use of information contained within.

For permission requests, write to the publisher, put in subject "Attention: Permissions Coordinator," at the address below, or contact us using our web site.

Aloha Library

Quantity sales or orders by U.S. trade bookstores and wholesalers. Special discounts are available on quantity purchases by corporations, associations, and others. For details, contact the publisher at the address above.

All books in this Million Book Edition by Aloha Library are in Public Domain. They are published first time before 1923, or before 1964 and copyright was not renewed.

Proudly Created in the United States of America

First Edition

19 18 17 16 15 / 10 9 8 7 6 5 4 3 2 1

Contents

Preface 5

Chapter 1

    Although it stands 6

Chapter 2

    It is said that 33

Chapter 3

    Lord Naoshige once said 46

Chapter 4

    When Nabeshima Tadanao 47

Chapter 6

    When Lord Takanobu 49

Chapter 7

    Narutomi Hyogo said 53

Chapter 8

    On the night of the thirteenth day 60

Chapter 9

    When Shimomura Shoun 71

Chapter 10

    There was a certain retainer 76

Chapter 11

    In the "Notes on Martial Laws" 85

Chapter 12

    Late night idle talk 93

PREFACE

Hagakure is the essential book of the Samurai. Written by Yamamoto Tsunetomo, who was a Samurai in the early 1700s, it is a book that combines the teachings of both Zen and Confucianism. These philosophies are centered on loyalty, devotion, purity and selflessness, and Yamamoto places a strong emphasis on the notion of living in the present moment with a strong and clear mind.

The Samurai were knights who defended and fought for their lords at a time when useful farming land was scarce and in need of protection. They believed in duty, and gave themselves completely to their masters. The Samurai believed that only after transcending all fear could they obtain peace of mind and yield the power to serve their masters faithfully and loyally even in the face of death.

The word Hagakure literally translates as hidden beneath the leaves and also fallen leaves. Perhaps it was named this because at the time that it was written, the way of the samurai was becoming obsolete.

The Hagakure has been rewritten in modern terms by one of Japan's famous writers, Yukio Mishima. His own views were very similar to those of Yamamoto, particularly the philosophy of cultivating the self. His characters all had self sufficiency in common, and did not rely upon anyone else for completion.

Although the Hagakure was written centuries ago for a breed of warriors that no longer exist, the philosophies and wisdom within are still practical, even in our modern times.

CHAPTER 1

Although it stands

ALTHOUGH it stands to reason that a samurai should be mindful of the Way of the Samurai, it would seem that we are all negligent. Consequently, if someone were to ask, "What is the true meaning of the Way of the Samurai?" the person who would be able to answer promptly is rare. This is because it has not been established in one's mind beforehand. From this, one's unmindfulness of the Way can be known.

Negligence is an extreme thing.

The Way of the Samurai is found in death. When it comes to either/or, there is only the quick choice of death. It is not particularly difficult. Be determined and advance. To say that dying without reaching one's aim is to die a dog's death is the frivolous way of sophisticates. When pressed with the choice of life or death, it is not necessary to gain one's aim.

We all want to live. And in large part we make our logic according to what we like. But not having attained our aim and continuing to live is cowardice. This is a thin dangerous line. To die without gaming one's aim is a dog's death and fanaticism. But there is no shame in this. This is the substance of the Way of the Samurai. If by setting one's heart right every morning and evening, one is able to live as though his body were already dead, he pains freedom in the Way. His whole life will be without blame, and he will succeed in his calling.

A man is a good retainer to the extent that he earnestly places importance in his master. This is the highest sort of retainer. If one is born into a prominent family that goes back for generations, it is sufficient to deeply consider the matter of obligation to one's ancestors, to lay down one's body and mind, and to earnestly esteem one's master. It is further good fortune if, more than this, one has wisdom and talent and can use them appropriately. But even a person who is good for nothing and exceedingly clumsy will be a reliable retainer if only he has the determination to think earnestly of his master. Having only wisdom and talent is the lowest tier of usefulness.

According to their nature, there are both people who have quick intelligence, and those who must withdraw and take time to think things over. Looking into this thoroughly, if one thinks selflessly and adheres to the four vows of the Nabeshima samurai, surprising wisdom will occur regardless of the high or low points of one's nature.

People think that they can clear up profound matters if they consider them deeply, but they exercise perverse thoughts and come to no good because they do their reflecting with only self-interest at the center.

It is difficult for a fool's habits to change to selflessness. In confronting a matter, however, if at first you leave it alone, fix the four vows in your heart, exclude self-interest, and make an effort, you will not go far from your mark.

Because we do most things relying only on our own sagacity we become self-interested, turn our backs on reason, and things do not turn out well. As seen by other people this is sordid, weak, narrow and inefficient. When one is not capable of true intelligence, it is good to consult with someone of good sense. An advisor will fulfill the Way when he makes a decision by selfless and frank intelligence because he is not personally involved.

This way of doing things will certainly be seen by others as being strongly rooted. It is, for example, like a large tree with many roots. One man's intelligence is like a tree that has been simply stuck in the ground.

We learn about the sayings and deeds of the men of old in order to entrust ourselves to their wisdom and prevent selfishness. When we throw off our own bias, follow the sayings of the ancients, and confer with other people, matters should go well and without mishap. Lord Katsushige borrowed from the wisdom of Lord Naoshige. This is mentioned in the Ohanashikikigaki. We should be grateful for his concern.

Moreover, there was a certain man who engaged a number of his younger brothers as retainers, and whenever he visited Edo or the Kamigata area, he would have them accompany him. As he consulted with them every day on both private and public matters, it is said that he was without mishap.

Sagara Kyuma was completely at one with his master and served him as though his own body were already dead. He was one man in a thousand.

Once there was an important meeting at Master Sakyo's Mizugae Villa, and it was commanded that Kyuma was to commit seppuku. At that time in Osaki there was a teahouse on the third floor of the suburban residence of Master Taku Nut.

Kyuma rented this, and gathering together all the good-for-nothings in Saga he put on a puppet show, operating one of the puppets himself, carousing and drinking all day and night. Thus, overlooking Master Sakyo's villa, he carried on and caused a great disturbance. In instigating this disaster he gallantly thought only of his master and was resolved to committing suicide.

Being a retainer is nothing other than hemp a supporter of one's lord, entrusting matters of good and evil to him, and renouncing self-interest. If there are but two or three men of this type, the fief will be secure.

If one looks at the world when affairs are going smoothly, there arc many who go about putting in their appearance, being useful by their wisdom, discrimination and artfulness. However, if the lord should retire or go into seclusion, there are many who will quickly turn their backs on him and ingratiate themselves to the man of the day. Such a thing is unpleasant even to think about. Men of high position, low position, deep wisdom and artfulness all feel that they are the ones who are working righteously, but when it comes to the point of throwing away one's life for his lord, all get weak in the knees. This is rather disgraceful. The fact that a useless person often becomes a matchless warrior at such times is because he has already given up his life and has become one with his lord. At the time of Mitsushige's death there was an example of this. His one resolved attendant was I alone. The others followed in my wake. Always the pretentious, self-asserting notables turn their backs on the man just as his eyes are closing in death.

Loyalty is said to be important in the pledge between lord and retainer. Though it may seem unobtainable, it is right before your eyes. If you once set yourself to it, you will become a superb retainer at that very moment.

To give a person one's opinion and correct his faults is an important thing. It is compassionate and comes first in matters of service. But the way of doing this is extremely difficult. To discover the good and bad points of a person is an easy thing, and to give an opinion concerning them is easy, too. For the most part, people think that they are being kind by saying the things that others find distasteful or difficult to say. But if it is not received well, they think that there is nothing more to be done. This is completely worthless. It is the same as brining shame to a person by slandering him. It is nothing more than getting it off one's chest.

To give a person an opinion one must first judge well whether that person is of the disposition to receive it or not. One must become close with him and make sure that he continually trusts one's word. Approaching subjects that are dear to him, seek the best way to speak and to be well understood. Judge the occasion, and determine whether it is better by letter or at the time of leave taking. Praise his good points and use every device to encourage him, perhaps by talking about one's own faults without touching on his, but so that they will occur to him. Have him receive this in the way that a man would drink water when his throat is dry, and it will be an opinion that will correct faults.

This is extremely difficult. If a person s fault is a habit of some years prior, by and large it won't be remedied. I have had this experience myself. To be intimate with alt one's comrades, correcting each other's faults, and being of one mind to be of use to the master is the great compassion of a retainer. By bringing shame to a person, bow could one expect to make him a better man?

It is bad taste to yawn in front of people. When one unexpectedly has to yawn, if he rubs his forehead in an upward direction, the sensation will stop. If that does not work, he can lick his lips while keeping his mouth closed, or simply hide it with his hand or his sleeve in such a way that no one will know what he is doing. It is the same with sneezing. One will appear foolish. There are other things besides these about which a person should use care and training. When a certain person was saying that present matters of economy should be detailed, someone replied that this is not good at all.

It is a fact that ash will not live where the water is too clear. But if there is duckweed or something, the fish will hide under its shadow and thrive. Thus, the lower classes will live in tranquility if certain matters are a bit overlooked or left unheard. This fact should be understood with regard to people's conduct.

Once when Lord Mitsushige was a little boy and was supposed to recite from a copybook for the priest Kaion, he called the other children and acolytes and said, "Please come here and listen. It's difficult to read if there are hardly any people listening." The priest was impressed and said to the acolytes, "That's the spirit in which to do everything."

Every morning one should first do reverence to his master and parents and then to his patron deities and guardian Buddhas. If he will only make his master first in importance, his parents will rejoice and the gods and Buddhas will give their assent. For a warrior there is nothing other than thinking of his master. If one creates this resolution within himself, he will always be mindful of the master's person and will not depart from him even for a moment.

Moreover, a woman should consider her husband first, just as he considers his master first.

According to a certain person, a number of years ago Matsuguma Kyoan told this story:

In the practice of medicine there is a differentiation of treatment according to the Yin and Yang of men and women. There is also a difference in pulse. In the last fifty years, however, men's pulse has become the same as women's. Noticing this, in the treatment of eye disease I applied women's treatment to men and found it suitable. When I observed the application of men's treatment to men, there was no result. Thus I knew that men's spirit had weakened and that they had become the same as women, and the end of the world had come. Since I witnessed this with certainty, I kept it a secret.

When looking at the men of today with this in mind, those who could be thought to have a woman's pulse are many indeed, and those who seem like real men few. Because of this, if one were to make a little effort, he would be able to take the upper hand quite easily. That there are few men who are able to cut well in beheadings is further proof that men's courage has waned. And when one comes to speak of kaishaku, it has become an age of men who are prudent and clever at making excuses. Forty or fifty years ago, when such things as matanuki were considered manly, a man wouldn't show an unscarred thigh to his fellows, so he would pierce it himself.

All of man's work is a bloody business. That fact, today, is considered foolish, affairs are finished cleverly with words alone, and jobs that require effort are avoided. I would like young men to have some understanding of this.

The priest Tannen used to say, "People come to no understanding because priests teach only the doctrine of 'No Mind.' What is called 'No Mind' is a mind that is pure and lacks complication.' This is interesting.

Lord Sanenori said, "In the midst of a single breath, where perversity cannot be held, is the Way. " If so, then the Way is one. But there is no one who can understand this clarity at first. Purity is something that cannot be attained except by piling effort upon effort.

There is nothing that we should be quite so grateful for as the last line of the poem that goes, "When your own heart asks." It can probably be thought of in the same way as the Nembutsu, and previously it was on the lips of many people.

Recently, people who are called "clever" adorn themselves with superficial wisdom and only deceive others. For this reason they are inferior to dull-wilted folk. A dull-wilted person is direct. If one looks deeply into his heart with the above phrase, there will be no hidden places. It is a good examiner. One should be of the mind that, meeting this examiner, he will not be embarrassed.

The word gen means "illusion" or "apparition." In India, a man who uses conjury is called a genjutsushi ["a master of illusion technique"]. Everything in this world is but a marionette show. Thus we use the word gen.

To hate injustice and stand on righteousness is a difficult thing. Furthermore, to think that being righteous is the best one can do and to do one's utmost to be righteous will, on the contrary, brig many mistakes. The Way is in a higher place then righteousness. This is very difficult to discover, but it is the highest wisdom. When seen from this standpoint, things like righteousness are rather shallow. If one does not understand this on his own, it cannot be known. There is a method of getting to this Way, however, even if one cannot discover it by himself. This is found in consultation with others. Even a person who has not attained this Way sees others front the side. It is like the saying from the game of go: "He who sees from the side has eight eyes." The saying, "Thought by thought we see our own mistakes," also means that the highest Way is in discussion with others. Listening to the old stories and reading books are for the purpose of sloughing off one's own discrimination and attaching oneself to that of the ancients.

A certain swordsman in his declining years said the following:

In one's life. there are levels in the pursuit of study. In the lowest level, a person studies but nothing comes of it, and he feels that both he and others are unskillful. At this point he is worthless. In the middle level he is still useless but is aware of his own insufficiencies and can also see the insufficiencies of others. In a higher level he has pride concerning his own ability, rejoices in praise from others, and laments the lack of ability in his fellows. This man has worth. In the highest level a man has the look of knowing nothing.

These are the levels in general;. But there is one transcending level, and this is the most excellent of all. This person is aware of the endlessness of entering deeply into a certain Way arid never thinks of himself as having finished. He truly knows his own insufficiencies and never in his whole life thinks that he has succeeded. He has no thoughts of pride but with self-abasement knows the Way to the end. It is said that Master Yagyu once remarked, "I do not know the way to defeat others, but the way to defeat myself."

Throughout your life advance daily, becoming more skillful than yesterday, more skillful than today. This is neverending.

Among the maxims on Lord Naoshige's wall there was this one: "Matters of' great concern should be treated lightly." Master Ittei commented, "Matters of small concern should be treated seriously." Among one's affairs there should not be more than two or three matters of what one could call great concern. If these are deliberated upon during ordinary times, they can be understood. Thinking about things previously and then handling them lightly when the time comes is what this is all about. To face an event anew solve it lightly is difficult if you are not resolved beforehand, and there will always be uncertainty in hitting your mark. However, if the foundation is laid previously, you can think of the saying, "Matters of great concern should be treated lightly," as your own basis for action.

A certain person spent several years of service in Osaka and then returned home. When he made his appearance at the local bureau, everyone was put out and he was made a laughingstock because he spoke in the Kamigata dialect. Seen in this light, when one spends a long time in ado or the Kamigata area, he had better use his native dialect even more than usual.

When in a more sophisticated area it is natural that one s disposition be affected by different styles. But it is vulgar and foolish to look down upon the ways of one's own district as being boorish, or to be even a bit open to the persuasion of the other place's ways and to think about giving up one's own.

That one's own district is unsophisticated and unpolished is a great treasure. Imitating another style is simply a sham.

A certain man said to the priest Shungaku, "The Lotus Sutra Sect's character is not good because it's so fearsome." Shungaku replied, "It is by reason of its fearsome character that it is the Lotus Sutra Sect. If its character were not so, it would be a different sect altogether." This is reasonable.

At the time when there was a council concerning the promotion of a certain man, the council members were at the point of deciding that promotion was useless because of the fact that the man had previously been involved in a drunken brawl. But someone said, "If we were to cast aside every man who had made a mistake once, useful men could probably not be come by. A man who makes a mistake once will be considerably more prudent and useful because of his repentance. I feel that he should be promoted."

Someone else then asked, "Will you guarantee him?" The man replied, "Of course I will."

The others asked, "By what will you guarantee him?"

And he replied, "I can guarantee him by the fact that he is a man who has erred once. A man who bas never once erred is dangerous." This said, the man was promoted.

At the time of a deliberation concerning criminals, Nakane Kazuma proposed making the punishment one degree lighter than what would be appropriate. This is a treasury of wisdom that only he was the possessor of. At that time, though there were several men in attendance, if it had not been for Kazuma alone, no one would have opened his mouth. For this reason he is called Master Commencement and Master Twenty-five Days.

A certain person was brought to shame because he did not take revenge. The way of revenge lies in simply forcing one's way into a place and being cut down. There is no shame in this. By thinking that you must complete the job you will run out of time. By considering things like how many men the enemy has, time piles up; in the end you will give up. No matter if the enemy has thousands of men, there is fulfillment in simply standing them off and being determined to cut them all down, starting from one end. You will finish the greater part of it.

Concerning the night assault of Lord Asano's ronin, the fact that they did not commit seppuku at the Sengakuji was an error, for there was a long delay between the time their lord was struck down and the time when they struck down the enemy. If Lord Kira had died of illness within that period, it would have been extremely regrettable. Because the men of the Kamigata area have a very clever sort of wisdom, they do well at praiseworthy acts but cannot do things indiscriminately, as was done in the Nagasaki fight.

Although all things are not to be judged in this manner, I mention it in the investigation of the Way of the Samurai. When the time comes, there is no moment for reasoning. And if you have not done your inquiring beforehand, there is most often shame. Reading books and listening to people's talk are for the purpose of prior resolution.

Above all, the Way of the Samurai should be in being aware that you do not know what is going to happen next, and in querying every item day and night. Victory and defeat are matters of the temporary force of circumstances. The way of avoiding shame is different. It is simply in death.

Even if it seems certain that you will lose, retaliate. Neither wisdom nor technique has a place in this. A real man does not think of victory or defeat. He plunges recklessly towards an irrational death. By doing this, you will awaken from your dreams.

There are two things that will blemish a retainer, and these are riches and honor. If one but remains in strained circumstances, he will not be marred.

Once there was a certain man who was very clever, but it was his character to always see the negative points of his jobs. In such a way, one will be useless. If one does not get it into his head from the very beginning that the world is full of unseemly situations, for the most part his demeanor will be poor and he will not be believed by others. And if one is not believed by others, no matter how good a person he may be, he will not have the essence of a good person. This can also be considered as a blemish.

There was a man who said, "Such and such a person has a violent disposition, but this is what I said right to his face... This was an unbecoming thing to say, and it was said simply because he wanted to be known as a rough fellow. It was rather low, and it can be seen that he was still rather immature. It is because a samurai has correct manners that he is admired. Speaking of other people in this way is no different from an exchange between low class spearmen. It is vulgar.

It is not good to settle into a set of opinions. It is a mistake to put forth effort and obtain some understanding and then stop at that. At first putting forth great effort to be sure that you have grasped the bastes, then practicing so that they may come to fruition is something that will never stop for your whole lifetime. Do not rely on following the degree of understanding that you have discovered, but simply think, "This is not enough." One should search throughout his whole life how best to follow the Way. And he should study, setting his mind to work without putting things off. Within this is the Way.

These are from the recorded sayings of Yamamoto Jin'emon:

- If you can understand one affair, you will understand eight.
- An affected laugh shows lack of self-respect in a man and lewdness in a woman.
- Whether speaking formally or informally, one should look his listener in the eye. A polite greeting is done at the beginning and finished. Speaking with downcast eyes is carelessness.

- It is carelessness to go about with one's hands inside the slits in the sides of his hakama.
- After reading books and the like, it is best to burn them or throw them away. It is said that reading books is the work of the Imperial Court, but the work of the House of Nakano is found in military valor, grasping the staff of oak.
- A samurai with no group and no horse is not a samurai at all.
- A kusemono is a man to rely upon. It is said that one should rise at four in the morning, bathe and arrange his hair daily, eat when the sun comes up, and retire when it becomes dark.
- A samurai will use a toothpick even though he has not eaten. Inside the skin of a dog, outside the hide of a tiger.

How should a person respond when he is asked, "As a human being, what is essential in terms of purpose and discipline?" First, let us say, "It is to become of the mind that is right now pure and lacking complications." People in general all seem to be dejected. When one has a pure and uncomplicated mind, his expression will be lively. When one is attending to matters, there is one thing that comes forth from his heart. That is, in terms of one's lord, loyalty; in terms of one's parents, filial piety; in martial affairs, bravery; and apart from that, something that can be used by all the world.

This is very difficult to discover. Once discovered, it is again difficult to keep in constant effect. There is nothing outside the thought of the immediate moment.

Every morning, the samurai of fifty or sixty years ago would bathe, shave their foreheads, put lotion in their hair, cut their fingernails and toenails rubbing them with pumice and then with wood sorrel, and without fail pay attention to their personal appearance. It goes without saying that their armor in general was kept free from rust, that it was dusted, shined, and arranged.

Although it seems that taking special care of one's appearance is similar to showiness, it is nothing akin to elegance. Even if you are aware that you may be struck down today and are firmly resolved to an inevitable death, if you are slain with an unseemly appearance, you will show your lack of previous resolve, will be despised by your enemy, and will appear unclean. For this reason it is said that both old and young should take care of their appearance.

Although you say that this is troublesome and time-consuming, a samurai's work is in such things. It is neither busy-work nor time-consuming. In constantly hardening one's resolution to die in battle, deliberately becoming as one already dead, and working at one's job and dealing with military affairs, there should be no shame. But when the time comes, a person will be shamed if he is not conscious of these things even in his dreams, and rather passes his days in self-interest and selfindulgence. And if he thinks that this is not shameful, and feels that nothing else matters as long as he is comfortable, then his dissipate and discourteous actions will be repeatedly regrettable.

The person without previous resolution to inevitable death makes certain that his death will be in bad form. But if one is resolved to death beforehand, in what way can he be despicable? One should be especially diligent in this concern.

Furthermore, during the last thirty years customs have changed; now when young samurai jeer together, if there is not just talk about money matters, loss and gain, secrets, clothing styles or matters of sex, there is no reason to gather together at all. Customs are going to pieces. One can say that formerly when a man reached the age of twenty or thirty, he did not carry despicable things in his heart, and thus neither did such words appear. If an elder unwittingly said something of that sort, he thought of it as a sort of injury. This new custom probably appears because people attach importance to being beautiful before society and to household finances. What things a person should be able to accomplish if he had no haughtiness concerning his place in society!

It is a wretched thing that the young men of today are so contriving and so proud of their material possessions. Men with contriving hearts are lacking in duty. Lacking in duty, they will have no self respect.

According to Master Ittei, even a poor penman will become substantial in the art of calligraphy if he studies by imitating a good model and puts forth effort. A retainer should be able to become substantial too, if he takes a good retainer as his model.

Today, however, there are no models of good retainers. In light of this, it would be good to make a model and to learn from that. To do this, one should look at many people and choose from each person his best point only. For example, one person for politeness, one for bravery, one for the proper way of speaking, one for correct conduct and one for steadiness of mind. Thus will the model be made.

An apprentice will not be up to his teacher's good points in the world of the arts either but will receive and imitate only his bad ones. This is worthless. There are people who are good at manners but have no uprightness. In imitating someone like this, one is likely to ignore the politeness and imitate only the lack of uprightness. If one perceives a person's good points, he will have a model teacher for anything.

When delivering something like an important letter or other written materials, grasp it firmly in your hand as you go and do not release it once, but hand it over directly to the recipient.

A retainer is a man who remains consistently undistracted twenty-four hours a day, whether he is in the presence of his master or in public. If one is careless during his rest period, the public will see him as being only careless.

Regardless of class, a person who does something beyond his social standing will at some point commit mean or cowardly acts. In the lower classes there are even people who will run away. One should be careful with menials and the like.

There are many people who, by being attached to a martial art and taking apprentices, believe that they have arrived at the full stature of a warrior. But it is a regrettable thing to put forth much effort and in the end become an "artist." In artistic technique it is good to learn to the extent that you will not be lacking. In general, a person who is versatile in many things is considered to be vulgar and to have only a broad knowledge of matters of importance.

When something is said to you by the master, whether it is for your good or bad fortune, to withdraw in silence shows perplexity. You should have some appropriate response. It is important to have resolution beforehand.

Moreover, if at the time that you are asked to perform some function you have deep happiness or great pride, it will show exactly as that on your face. This has been seen in many people and is rather unbecoming. But another type of person knows his own defects and thinks, "I'm a clumsy person but I've been asked to do this thing anyway. Now how am I going to go about it? I can see that this is going to be much trouble and cause for concern." Though these words are never said, they will appear on the surface. This shows modesty.

By inconsistency and frivolity we stray from the Way and show ourselves to be beginners. In this we do much harm.

Learning is a good thing, but more often it leads to mistakes. It is like the admonition of the priest Konan. It is worthwhile just looking at the deeds of accomplished persons for the purpose of knowing our own insufficiencies. But often this does not happen. For the most part, we admire our own opinions and become fond of arguing.

Last year at a great conference there was a certain man who explained his dissenting opinion and said that he was resolved to kill the conference leader if it was not accepted. His motion was passed. After the procedures were over the man said, "Their assent came quickly. I think that they are too weak and unreliable to be counselors to the master."

When an official place is extremely busy and someone comes in thoughtlessly with some business or other, often there are people who will treat him coldly and become angry. This is not good at all. At such times, the etiquette of a samurai is to calm himself and deal with the person in a good manner. To treat a person harshly is the way of middle class lackeys.

According to the situation, there are times when you must rely on a person for something or other. If this is done repeatedly, it becomes a matter of importuning that person and can be rather rude. If there is something that must be done, it is better not to rely on others.

There is something to be learned from a rainstorm. When meeting with a sudden shower, you try not to pet wet and run quickly along the road. But doing such things as passing under the eaves of houses, you still get wet. When you are resolved from the beginning, you will not be perplexed, though you still get the same soaking. This understanding extends to everything.

In China there was once a man who liked pictures of dragons, and his clothing and furnishings were all designed accordingly. His deep affection for dragons was brought to the attention of the dragon god, and one day a real dragon appeared before his window. It is said that he died of fright. He was probably a man who always spoke big words but acted differently when facing the real thing.

There was a certain person who was a master of the spear. When he was dying, he called his best disciple and spoke his last injunctions:

I have passed on to you all the secret techniques of this school, and there is nothing left to say. If you think of taking on a disciple yourself, then you should practice diligently with the bamboo sword every day. Superiority is not just a matter of secret techniques.

Also, in the instructions of a renga teacher, it was said that the day before the poetry meeting one should calm his mind and look at a collection of poems. This is concentration on one affair. All professions should be done with concentration.

Although the Mean is the standard for all things, in military affairs a man must always strive to outstrip others. According to archery instructions the right and left hands are supposed to be level, but the right hand has a tendency to go higher. They will become level if one will lower the right hand a bit when shooting. In the stories of the elder warriors it is said that on the battlefield if one wills himself to outstrip warriors of accomplishment, and day and night hopes to strike down a powerful enemy, he will grow indefatigable and fierce of heart and will manifest courage. One should use this principle in everyday affairs too.

There is a way of bringing up the child of a samurai. From the time of infancy one should encourage bravery and avoid trivially frightening or teasing the child. If a person is affected by cowardice as a child, it remains a lifetime scar. It is a mistake for parents to thoughtlessly make their children dread lightning, or to have them not go into dark places, or to tell them frightening things in order to stop them from crying.

Furthermore, a child will become timid if he is scolded severely.

One should not allow bad habits to form. After a bad habit is ingrained, although you admonish the child he will not improve. As for such things as proper speaking and good manners, gradually make the child aware of them. Let him not know avarice. Other than that, if he is of a normal nature, he should develop well by the way he is brought up.

Moreover, the child of parents who have a bad relationship will be unfilial. This is natural. Even the birds and beasts are affected by what they are used to seeing and hearing from the time they are born. Also, the relationship between father and child may deteriorate because of a mother's foolishness. A mother loves her child above all things, and will be partial to the child that is corrected by his father. If she becomes the child's ally, there will be discord between father and son. Because of the shallowness of her mind, a woman sees the child as her support in old age.

You will be tripped up by people when your resolution is lax. Moreover, if at a meeting you are distracted while another person is speaking, by your carelessness you may think that he is of your opinion and you will follow along saying, "Of course, of course," even though he is saying something that is contrary to your own feelings, and others will think that you are in agreement with him. Because of this, you should never be distracted even for an instant when meeting with others.

When you are listening to a story or being spoken to, you should be mindful not to be tripped up; and if there is something that you do not agree with, to speak your mind, to show your opponent his error, and to grapple with the situation. Even in unimportant affairs mistakes come from little things. One should be mindful of this. Moreover, it is better not to become acquainted with men about whom you have formerly had some doubts. No matter what you do, they will be people by whom you will be tripped up or taken in, To be certain of this fact you must have much experience.

The saying, "The arts aid the body," is for samurai of other regions. For samurai of the Nabeshima clan the arts bring ruin to the body. In all cases, the person who practices an art is an artist, not a samurai, and one should have the intention of being called a samurai.

When one has the conviction that even the slightest artful ability is harmful to the samurai, all the arts become useful to him. One should understand this sort of thing.

Ordinarily, looking into the mirror and grooming oneself is sufficient for the upkeep of one's personal appearance. This is very important. Most people's personal appearance is poor because they do not look into the mirror well enough.

Training to speak properly can be done by correcting one's speech when at home.

Practice in letter writing goes to the extent of taking care in even one-line letters.

It is good if all the above contain a quiet strength. Moreover, according to what the priest Ryozan heard when he was in the Kamgala area, when one is writing a letter, he should think that the recipient will make it into a hanging scroll.

It is said that one should not hesitate to correct himself when he has made a mistake. If he corrects himself without the least bit of delay, his mistakes will quickly disappear. But when he tries to cover up a mistake, it will become all the more unbecoming and painful. When words that one should not use slip out, if one will speak his mind quickly and clearly, those words will have no effect and he will not be obstructed by worry. If there is, however, someone who blames a person for such a thing, one should be prepared to say something like, "I have explained the reason for my careless speech. There is nothing else to be done if you will not listen to reason. Since I said it unwittingly, it should be the same as if you didn't hear it. No one can evade blame." And one should never talk about people or secret matters. Furthermore, one should only speak according to how he judges his listener's feelings.

The proper manner of calligraphy is nothing other than not being careless, but in this way one's writing will simply be sluggish and stiff.

One should go beyond this and depart from the norm. This principle applies to all things.

It is said, "When you would see into a person's heart, become ill." When you are sick or in difficulties, many of those who were friendly or close to you in daily life will become cowards. Whenever anyone is in unhappy circumstances, you should above all inquire after them by visiting or sending some gift. And you should never in your whole life be negligent toward someone from whom you have received a favor.

By such things the consideration of others can be seen. In this world the people who will rely on others when they are in difficulties and afterwards not give them a thought are many.

You cannot tell whether a person is good or bad by his vicissitudes in life. Good and bad fortune are matters of fate. Good and bad actions are Man's Way. Retribution of good and evil is taught simply as a moral lesson.

Because of some business, Morooka Hikoemon was called upon to swear before the gods concerning the truth of a certain matter. But he said, "A samurai's word is harder than metal. Since I have impressed this fact upon myself, what more can the gods and Buddhas do?" and the swearing was cancelled. This happened when he was twenty-six.

Master Ittei said, "Whatever one prays for will be granted. Long ago there were no matsutake mushrooms in our province. Some men who saw them in the Kamigata area prayed that they might grow here, and nowadays they are growing all over Kitagama. In the future I would like to have Japanese cypress grow in our province. As this is something that everyone desires, I predict it for the future. This being so, everyone should pray for it."

When something out of the ordinary happens, it is ridiculous to say that it is a mystery or a portent of something to come. Eclipses of the sun and moon, comets, clouds that flutter like flags, snow in the fifth month, lightning in the twelfth month, and so on, are all things that occur every fifty or one hundred years. They occur according to the evolution of Yin and Yang. The fact that the sun rises in the east and sets in the west would be a mystery, too, if it were not an everyday occurrence.

It is not dissimilar. Furthermore, the fact that something bad always happens in the world when strange phenomena occur is due to people seeing something like fluttering clouds and thinking that something is going to happen. The mystery is created in their minds, and by waiting for the disaster, it is from their very minds that it occurs. The occurrence of mysteries is always by word of mouth.

Calculating people are contemptible. The reason for this is that calculation deals with loss and pain, and the loss and gain mind never stops. Death is considered loss and life is considered gain. Thus, death is something that such a person does not care for, and he is contemptible.

Furthermore, scholars and their like are men who with wit and speech hide their own true cowardice and greed. People often misjudge this.

Lord Naoshige said, "The Way of the Samurai is in desperateness. Ten men or more cannot kill such a man. Common sense will not accomplish great things. Simply become insane and desperate.' "In the Way of the Samurai, if one uses discrimination, he will fall behind. One needs neither loyalty nor devotion, but simply to become desperate in the Way. Loyalty and devotion are of themselves within desperation."

The saying of Shida Kichinosuke, "When there is a choice of either living or dying, as long as there remains nothing behind to blemish one's reputation, it is better to live," is a paradox. He also said, "When there is a choice of either going or not going, it is better not to go." A corollary to this would he, "When there is a choice of either eating or not eating, it is better not to eat.

When there is a choice of either dying or not dying, it is better to die."

When meeting calamities or difficult situations, it is not enough to simply say that one is not at all flustered. When meeting difficult situations, one should dash forward bravely and with joy. It is the crossing of a single barrier and is like the saying, "The more the water, the higher the boat."

It is spiritless to think that you cannot attain to that which you have seen and heard the masters attain. The masters are men. You are also a man. If you think that you will be inferior in doing something, you will be on that road very soon. Master Ittei said, "Confucius was a sage because he had the will to become a scholar when he was fifteen years old. He was not a sage because he studied later on." This is the same as the Buddhist maxim, "First intention, then enlightenment."

A warrior should be careful in all things and should dislike to be the least bit worsted. Above all, if he is not careful in his choice of words he may say things like, "I'm a coward," or "At that time I'd probably run," or "How frightening," or "How painful." These are words that should not be said even in jest, on a whim, or when talking in one's sleep. If a person with understanding hears such things, he will see to the bottom of the speaker's heart. This is something that should be carefully thought about beforehand.

When one's own attitude on courage is fixed in his heart, and when his resolution is devoid of doubt, then when the time comes he will of necessity be able to choose the right move. This will be manifested by one's conduct and speech according to the occasion. One's word is especially important. It is not for exposing the depths of one's heart. This is something that people will know by one's everyday affairs.

After I took up the attitude of a retainer, I never sat sloppily whether at home or in some other place. Neither did I speak, but if there was something that could not be done properly without words, I made an effort to settle things by putting ten words into one. Yamazaki Kurando was like this.

It is said that even after one's head has been cut off, he can still perform some function. This fact can be known from the examples of Nitta Yoshisada and Ono Doken. How shall one man be inferior to another? Mitani Jokyu said, "Even if a man be sick to death, he can bear up for two or three days."

In the words of the ancients, one should make his decisions within the space of seven breaths. Lord Takanobu said, "If discrimination is long, it will spoil." Lord Naoshige said, "When matters are done leisurely, seven out of ten will turn out badly. A warrior is a person who does things quickly."

When your mind is going hither and thither, discrimination will never be brought to a conclusion. With an intense, fresh and undelaying spirit, one will make his judgments within the space of seven breaths. It is a matter of being determined and having the spirit to break right through to the other side.

In admonishing the master, if one is not of the proper rank to do so, it shows great loyalty to have someone who is of that rank speak and have the master correct his mistakes. To be on a footing to do this one must be on cordial terms with everyone. If one does this for his own sake, it is simply flattery. One does this, rather, in his concern to support the clan on his own. If one will do it, it can be done.

Bad relations between retired and present rulers, father and son, and elder and younger brothers develop from selfish motives. The proof of this is that there are no such bad relations between master and retainer.

It is unthinkable to be disturbed at something like being ordered to become a ronin. People at the time of Lord Katsushige used to say, "If one has not been a ronin at least seven times, he will not be a true retainer. Seven times down, eight times up."

Men like Narutomi Hyogo have been ronin seven times. One should understand that it is something like being a self righting doll. The master is also apt to give such orders as a test.

Illnesses and the like become serious because of one's feelings. I was born when my father was seventy-one years old and was hence a rather sickly child. But because I have had the great desire to be of use even in old age, when the chance came I improved my health and haven't been sick since.

And I have abstained from sex and have consistently taken moxa cautery. There are things that I feel have definitely had effect.

There is a saying that even though one burns up a mamushi seven times, it will return each time to its original form. This is my great hope. I have always been obsessed with one idea: to be able to realize my heart's desire, which is that, though I am born seven times, each time I will be reborn as a retainer of my clan.

Yamamoto Jin'emon once said that it is best for a samurai to have good retainers. Military affairs are not matters for one person alone, regardless of how useful he tries to be. Money is something that one can borrow from people, but a good man cannot suddenly be come by. One should sustain a man kindly and well from the first. And in having retainers it will not do to nourish oneself alone. If you divide what you have and feed your lower ranks, you will be able to hold good men.

A person with a bit of wisdom is one who will criticize the times. This is the basis of disaster. A person who is discreet in speaking will be useful during the good times and will avoid punishment during the bad.

Being superior to others is nothing other than having people talk about your affairs and listening to their opinions. The general run of people settle for their own opinions and thus never excel. Having a discussion with a person is one step in excelling him, A certain person discussed with me the written materials at the clan office. He is better than someone like me in writing and researching. In seeking correction from others, you excel them.

It is bad when one thing becomes two. One should not look for anything else in the Way of the Samurai. It is the same for anything that is called a Way. Therefore, it is inconsistent to hear something of the Way of Confucius or the Way of the Buddha, and say that this is the Way of the Samurai. If one understands things in this manner, he should be able to hear about all Ways and be more and more in accord with his own.

For a samurai, a simple word is important no matter where he may be. By just one single word martial valor can be made apparent. In peaceful times words show one's bravery. In troubled times, too, one knows that by a single word his strength or cowardice can be seen. This single word is the flower of one's heart. It is not something said simply with one's mouth.

A warrior should not say something fainthearted even casually. He should set his mind to this beforehand. Even in trifling matters the depths of one's heart can be seen.

No matter what it is, there is nothing that cannot be done. If one manifests the determination, he can move heaven and earth as he pleases. But because man is pluckless, he cannot set his mind to it. Moving heaven and earth without putting forth effort is simply a matter of concentration.

A person who is said to be proficient at the arts is like a fool. Because of his foolishness in concerning himself with just one thing, he thinks of nothing else and thus becomes proficient. He is a worthless person.

Until the age of forty it is best to gather strength. It is appropriate to have settled down by the age of fifty.

When discussing things with someone, it is best to speak appropriately about whatever the subject may be. No matter how good what you are saying might be, it will dampen the conversation if it is irrelevant.

When someone is giving you his opinion, you should receive it with deep gratitude even though it is worthless. If you don't, he will not tell you the things that he has seen and heard about you again. It is best to both give and receive opinions in a friendly way.

There is a saying that great genius matures late. If something is not brought to fruition over a period of twenty to thirty years, it will not be of great merit. When a retainer is of a mind to do his work hurriedly, he will intrude upon the work of others and will be said to be young but able. He will become over enthusiastic and will be considered rather rude. He will put on the airs of someone who has done great works, will become a flatterer and insincere, and will be talked about behind his back. In the pursuit of one's development, if he does not make great effort and is not supported by others in his advancement in the world, he will be of no use.

When one is involved in the affairs of a warrior such as being a kaishaku or making an arrest within one's own clan or group, people will notice when the time comes if he has resolved beforehand that no one can take his place. One should always take the attitude of standing above others in martial valor, always feel that he is inferior to no one, and always cultivate his courage.

When on the battlefield, if you try not to let others take the lead and have the sole intention of breaking into the enemy lines, then you will not fall behind others, your mind will become fierce, and you will manifest martial valor. This fact has been passed down by the elders. Furthermore, if you are slain in battle, you should be resolved to have your corpse facing the enemy.

If everyone were in accord and left things to Providence, their hearts would be at ease. If they are not in accord, though they would do acts of righteousness, they lack loyalty. To be at odds with one's companions, to be prone to miss even infrequent meetings, to speak only cantankerous words—all come from a shallow foolishness of mind. But thinking of the moment of truth, even though it be unpleasant, one should fix it in his mind to meet people cordially at all times and without distraction, and in a way in which one will not seem bored. Moreover, in this world of uncertainties one is not even sure of the present. It would be worthless to die while being thought ill of by people. Lies and insincerity are unbecoming. This is because they are for self profit.

Though it is not profitable to have others lead the way, or not to be quarrelsome, or not to be lacking in manners, or to be humble, if one will do things for the benefit of others and meet even those whom he has met often before in a first-time manner, he will have no bad relationships. Manners between husband and wife are not different from this. If one is as discreet in the end as he is in the beginning, there should be no discord.

There is a certain priest who is said to be able to get everything accomplished by means of his cleverness. There is not a monk in japan today who can oppose him. This is not the least bit strange. There is simply no one who sees through to the foundation of things.

Senility is when one goes about doing only that towards which he is most inclined. One is able to suppress and hide this while his vigor is still strong, but when he weakens, the essential strong points of his nature appear and are a shame to him. This manifests itself in several forms, but there is not a man who does not get senile by the time he reaches sixty. And when one thinks that he will not be senile, he is already so, It can be thought that Master Ittei had a senility of argumentation. As if to show that he alone could support the House of Nabeshima, he went about with a senile appearance to prominent people's houses and chatted amiably with them. At the time, everybody thought that it was reasonable, but thinking about it now, it was senility. For myself, with that good example and the feeling that dotage was overtaking me, I declined to participate at the temple on the thirteenth anniversary of Lord Mitsushige's death, and I have decided to stay more and more indoors. One must get a clear view of what lies ahead.

If one is but secure at the foundation, he will not be pained by departure from minor details or affairs that are contrary to expectation. But in the end, the details of a matter are important. The right and wrong of one's way of doing things are found in trivial matters.

According to a story at the Ryutaiji, there was a master of the Book of Changes in the Kamigata area who said that even if a man is a priest, it is useless to give him rank while he is under the ape of forty. This is because he will make many mistakes. Confucius was not the only man to become unperplexed after reaching the age of forty. Upon reaching the age of forty, both wise and foolish have gone through an appropriate amount of experience and will no longer be perplexed.

Concerning martial valor, merit lies more in dying for one's master than in striking down the enemy. This can be understood from the devotion of Sate Tsugunobu.

When I was young, I kept a "Dairy of Regret" and tried to record my mistakes day by day, but there was never a day when I didn't have twenty or thirty entries. As there was no end to it, I gave up. Even today, when I think about the day's affairs after going to bed, there is never a day when I do not make some blunder in speaking or in some activity. Living without mistakes is truly impossible. But this is something that people who live by cleverness have no inclination to think about.

When reading something aloud, it is best to read from the belly. Reading from one's mouth, one's voice will not endure. This is Nakano Shikibu's teaching.

During happy times, pride and extravagance are dangerous. If one is not prudent in ordinary times, he will not be able to catch up. A person who advances during good times will falter during the bad.

Master Ittei said, "In calligraphy it is progress when the paper, brush and ink are in harmony." Yet they are so wont to be disjointed!

The master took a book from its box. When he opened it there was the smell of drying clovebuds.

What is called generosity is really compassion. In the Shin'ei it is written, "Seen from the eye of compassion, there is no one to be disliked. One who has sinned is to be pitied all the more." There is no limit to the breadth and depth of one's heart. There is room enough for all. That we still worship the sages of the three ancient kingdoms is because their compassion reaches us yet today.

Whatever you do should be done for the sake of your master and parents, the people in general, and for posterity. This is great compassion. The wisdom and courage that come from compassion are real wisdom and courage. When one punishes or strives with the heart of compassion, what he does will be limitless in strength and correctness. Doing something for one's own sake is shallow and mean and turns into evil. I understood the matters of wisdom and courage some time ago. I am just now beginning to understand the matter of compassion.

Lord Ieyasu said, "The foundation for ruling the country in peace is compassion, for when one thinks of the people as being his children, the people will think of him as their parent." Moreover, can't it be thought that the names "group parent" and "group child" [i.e., group leader and member] are so called because they are attached to each other by the harmonious hearts of a parent-child relationship?

One can understand that Lord Naoshige's phrase, "A faultfinder will come to be punished by others," came from his compassion. His saying, "Principle is beyond reason," should also be considered compassion. He enthusiastically stated that we should taste the inexhaustible.

The priest Tannen said, "A clever retainer will not advance. However, there are no cases of stupid people coming up in the world either."

This was Nakano Shikibu's opinion.

When one is young, he can often bring on shame for a lifetime by homosexual acts. To have no understanding of this is dangerous. As there is no one to inform young men of this matter, I can give its general outline.

One should understand that a woman is faithful to only one husband. Our feelings go to one person for one lifetime. If this is not so, it is the same as sodomy or prostitution. This is shame for a warrior. Ihara Saikaku has written a famous line that goes, "An adolescent without an older lover is the same as a woman with no husband." But this sort of person is ridiculous.

A young man should test an older man for at least five years, and if he is assured of that person's intentions, then he too should request the relationship. A fickle person will not enter deeply into a relationship and later will abandon his lover.

If they can assist and devote their lives to each other, then their nature can be ascertained. But if one partner is crooked, the other should say that there are hindrances to the relationship and sever it with firmness. If the first should ask what those hindrances are, then one should respond that he will never in his life say. If he should continue to push the matter, one should get angry; if he continues to push even further, cut him down.

Furthermore, the older man should ascertain the younger's real motives in the aforementioned way. If the younger man can devote himself and pet into the situation for five or six years, then it will not be unsuitable.

Above all, one should not divide one's way into two. One should strive in the Way of the Samurai.

Hoshino Ryotetsu was the progenitor of homosexuality in our province, and although it can be said that his disciples were many, he instructed each one individually. Edayoshi Saburozaemon was a man who understood the foundation of homosexuality. Once, when accompanying his master to ado, Ryotetsu asked Saburozaemon, "What have you understood of homosexuality?"

Saburozaemon replied, "It is something both pleasant and unpleasant."

Ryotetsu was pleased and said, "You have taken great pains for some time to be able to say such a thing."

Some years later there was a person who asked Saburozaemen the meaning of the above. He replied, "To lay down one's life for another is the basic principle of homosexuality. If it is not so, it becomes a matter of shame. However, then you have nothing left to lay down for your master. It is therefore understood to be something both pleasant and unpleasant."

Master Ittei said, ' 'If one were to say what it is to do good, in a single word it would be to endure suffering. Not enduring is bad without exception."

Until one reaches the ape of forty it is better to put off wisdom and discrimination and excel in vitality. According to the person and the rank, though a person has passed the age of forty, if he has no vitality, he will pet no response from others.

Recently, a certain person on his way to Edo sent home a detailed letter from the first night's inn. Though he was a person who neglected such things when he was busy, he excelled other people in being as attentive as this.

In the judgment of the elders, a samurai's obstinacy should be excessive. A thing done with moderation may later be judged to be insufficient. I have heard that when one thinks he has gone too far, he will not have erred. This sort of rule should not be forgotten.

When one has made a decision to kill a person, even if it will be very difficult to succeed by advancing straight ahead, it will not do to think about going at it in a long roundabout way. One's heart may slacken, he may miss his chance, and by and large there will be no success. The Way of the Samurai is one of immediacy, and it is best to dash in headlong. When a certain man was going to the sutra readings at the Jissoin in Kawakami, one of his pages got drunk on the ferryboat and began to pester one of the sailors. When they landed on the other side, as the page had drawn his sword, the sailor took a pole and struck him on the head. At that time the other sailors all ran up together carrying oars and were at the point of striking the page down. However, as the master passed by with an air of not knowing what was happening, one of the other pages ran back and apologized to the sailors. Then, pacifying his comrade, he accompanied him home. That night the page who had been drunk learned that his sword was being taken away from him.

Now, first of all, it was an insufficiency on the master's part not to have reproved and pacified the drunken page while they were on the boat. Furthermore, even though his page had acted unreasonably, after he had been struck on the head there was no reason for an apology. The master should have approached the sailor and the drunken page in an apologetic manner and cut them both down. Certainly he was a spiritless master.

The resolution of the men of former times was deep. Those between the ages of thirteen and sixty went to the front lines. For this reason men of advanced years hid their age.

For serious affairs that bear directly on oneself, if one does not take care of things by making his own judgment his foundation and breaking through headlong, matters will not be brought to a close. In conferring with people about matters of importance, there may be many cases when your affair is thought lightly of, or when people will not speak of the real circumstances. At such times one must use his own judgment. At any rate, it is sufficient to become a fanatic and choose to throw away one's life. At such a time, if one thinks about doing things well, confusion will soon arise and he will blunder. In many cases one's downfall may be brought about by an ally who is trying to do something for one's benefit, or one may be killed by his friend's kindness. It is the same as when one requests permission to become a monk.

Lord Naoshige said, "An ancestor's good or evil can be determined by the conduct of his descendants." A descendant should act in a way that will manifest the good in his ancestor and not the bad. This is filial piety.

It is a wretched thing that one's family lineage be thrown into confusion with an adoption based on money alone. Such a thing is immoral from the beginning, but it is extreme wickedness to be thus immoral with the excuse that without doing so one will be unable to afford even today's rice.

When Nakano Shogen committed seppuku, the members of his group gathered at Oki Hyobu's place and said various bad things about him. Hyobu said, "One does not speak bad things about a person after his death. And especially since a person who has received some censure is to be pitied, it is the obligation of a samurai to speak something good of him, no matter how little. There is no doubt that in twenty years Shogen will have the reputation of a faithful retainer." These were truly the words of a seasoned man.

To place one's armor out splendidly is a fine discipline, but it is sufficient if it is simply all accounted for. Fukabori Inosuke 's armor is a good example. Men of high rank and with many retainers will also need such things as money to set aside for campaign use. It is said that Okabe Kunai made bags equaling the number of men in his;group, affixed a name to each, and put in the appropriate amount of money for a campaign. This sort of discipline is profound. As for men of low rank, if they cannot make the proper preparation at the time, they should rely on assistance from their group leader. To this extent, it is necessary for the group leader to be on intimate terms with his men beforehand. As for men who are under the master's direction, and especially for those who are with him directly, it is better to be without preparation money. At the time of the summer maneuvers at Osaka, a certain person brought along twelve monme of refined silver and went off with Master Taku Zusho. This, of course, would have been fine if he had simply ridden off early. I think that it is better to dispense with such care.

In carefully scrutinizing the affairs of the past, we find that there are many different opinions about them, and that there are some things that are quite unclear. It is better to regard such things as unknowable. Lord Sanenori once said, "As for the things that we don't understand, there are ways of understanding them. Furthermore, there are some things we understand just naturally, and again some that we can't understand no matter how hard we try. This is interesting."

This is very profound. It is natural that one cannot understand deep and hidden things. Those things that are easily understood are rather shallow.

CHAPTER 2

It is said that

IT is SAID that much sake, self-pride and luxury are to be avoided by a samurai, There is no cause for anxiety when you are unhappy, but when you become a little elated, these three things become dangerous. Look at the human condition. It is unseemly for a person to become prideful and extravagant when things are going well. Therefore, it is better to have some unhappiness while one is still young, for if a person does not experience some bitterness, his disposition will not settle down. A person who becomes fatigued when unhappy is useless.

Meeting with people should be a matter of quickly grasping their temperament and reacting appropriately to this person and that. Especially with an extremely argumentative person, after yielding considerably one should argue him down with superior logic, but without sounding harsh, and in a fashion that will allow no resentment to be left afterwards. This is a function of both the heart and words. This was an opinion given by a priest concerning personal encounters.

Dreams are truthful manifestations. When I occasionally have dreams of dying in battle or committing seppuku, if I brace myself with courage, my frame of mind within the dream gradually changes.

This concerns the dream I had on the night of the twenty-seventh day of the fifth month.

If one were to say in a word what the condition of being a samurai is, its basis lies first in seriously devoting one's body and soul to his master. And if one is asked what to do beyond this, it would be to fit oneself inwardly with intelligence, humanity and courage.' The combining of these three virtues may seem unobtainable to the ordinary person, but it is easy. Intelligence is nothing more than discussing things with others. Limitless wisdom comes from this. Humanity is something done for the sake of others, simply comparing oneself with them and putting them in the fore. Courage is gritting one' s teeth; it is simply doing that and pushing ahead, paying no attention to the circumstances. Anything that seems above these three is not necessary to be known.

As for outward aspects, there are personal appearance, one's way of speaking and calligraphy. And as all of these are daily matters, they improve by constant practice. Basically, one should perceive their nature to be one of quiet strength. If one has accomplished all these things, then he should have a knowledge of our area's history and customs. After that he may study the various arts as recreation. If you think it over, being a retainer is simple. And these days, if you observe people who are even a bit useful, you will see that they have accomplished these three outward aspects.

A certain priest said that if one thoughtlessly crosses a river of unknown depths and shallows, he will die in its currents without ever reaching the other side or finishing his business. This is the same as when one is indiscriminately eager in being a retainer without understanding the customs of the times or the likes and dislikes of the master and, as a result, is of no use and brings ruin upon himself. To try to enter the good graces of the master is unbecoming. One should consider first stepping back and getting some understanding of the depths and shallows and then work without doing anything the master dislikes.

If you attach a number of bags of cloves to your body, you will not be affected by inclemency or colds. Some years ago Nakano Kazuma returned to this province as a messenger by horse in the dead of winter, and though he was an old man, he was not the least bit in pain. It is said that that was because of his having used cloves. Furthermore, drinking a decoction of the feces from a dappled horse is the way to stop bleeding from an injury received by falling off a horse.

A faultless person is one who withdraws from affairs. This must be done with strength.

There is surely nothing other than the single purpose of the present moment. A man's whole life is a succession of moment after moment. If one fully understands the present moment, there will be nothing else to do, and nothing else to pursue. Live being true to the single purpose of the moment.

Everyone lets the present moment slip by, then looks for it as though he thought it were somewhere else. No one seems to have noticed this fact. But grasping this firmly, one must pile experience upon experience. And once one has come to this understanding he will be a different person from that point on, though he may not always bear it in mind.

When one understands this settling into single-mindedness well, his affairs will thin out. Loyalty is also contained within this single-mindedness.

It is said that what is called "the spirit of an ape' ' is seinething to which one cannot return. That this spirit gradually dissipates is due to the world's coming to an end. In the same way, a single year does not have just spring or summer. A single day, too, is the same.

For this reason, although one would like to change today's world back to the spirit of one hundred years or more ago, it cannot be done. Thus it is important to make the best out of every generation. This is the mistake of people who are attached to past generations. They have no understanding of this point.

On the other hand, people who only know the disposition of the present day and dislike the ways of the past are too lax.

Be true to the thought of the moment and avoid distraction. Other than continuing to exert yourself, enter into nothing else, but go to the extent of living single thought by single thought.

The brave men of old times were for the most part rowdies. As they were of the disposition to be out running amuck, their vitality was strong and they were brave. When I had doubts about this and asked, Tsunetomo said, "It is understandable that since their vitality was strong they were generally rough and went about running amuck. These days rowdiness is nonexistent because man's vitality has weakened. Vitality has fallen behind, but man's character has improved. Valor is yet a different thing. Although men have become gentle these days because of the lack of vitality, this does not mean that they are inferior in being crazy to die. That has nothing to do with vitality."

Concerning the military tactics of Lord Naoshige, Ushida Shoemon said that it was characteristic of his retainers to face a situation with no previous knowledge of what was to happen, and for him to freely bring everything to a finish by a single word. When he was at the point of passing from this world, he said nothing, even when his chief retainers came to see him.

Once Lord Ieyasu gamed nothing in a battle, but in a later judgment it was said, "Ieyasu is a general of great courage. Of his retainers who died in battle, not one of them died with his back turned. They all died facing the enemy lines." Since a warrior's daily frame of mind is manifested even after death, it is something that can bring shame to him.

As Yasuda Ukyo said about offering up the last wine cup, only the end of things is important. One's whole life should be like this. When guests are leaving, the mood of being reluctant to say farewell is essential. If this mood is lacking, one will appear bored and the day and evening's conversation will disappear. In all dealings with people it is essential to have a fresh approach. One should constantly give the impression that he is doing something exceptional. It is said that this is possible with but a little understanding.

Our bodies are given life from the midst of nothingness. Existing where there is nothing is the meaning of the phrase, "Form is emptiness." That all things are provided for by nothingness is the meaning of the phrase, "Emptiness is form."' One should not think that these are two separate things.

Uesugi Kenshin said, "I never knew about winning from beginning to end, but only about not being behind in a situation." This is interesting. A retainer will be dumbfounded if he is behind in a situation. In each and every instance one's function or responsiveness will not be shallow if he is not behind.

One should be wary of talking on end about such subjects as learning, morality or folklore in front of elders or people of rank. It is disagreeable to listen to.

In the Kamigata area they have a sort of tiered lunch box they use for a single day when flower viewing. Upon returning, they throw them away, trampling them underfoot. As might be expected, this is one of my recollections of the capital [Kyoto]. The end is important in all things.

While walking along the road together, Tsunetomo said, "Is not man like a welloperated puppet? It is a piece of dexterous workmanship that he can run, jump, leap, and even talk though there are no strings attached. Will we not be guests at next year's Ben Festival? This world is vanity indeed. People always forget this."

It was once said to one of the young lords that "right now" is "at that time, " and "at that time" is "right now." One will miss the occasion if he thinks that these two are different. For example, if one were called before the master to explain something right away, he would most likely be perplexed. This is proof that he understands the two to be different. If, however, a person makes "right now" and "at that time" one, though he will never be an advisor to the master, still he is a retainer, and in order to be able to say something clearly, whether it be in front of the master, the elders or even the shogun at Edo Castle, it should be practiced beforehand in the corner of one's bedroom.

All things are like this. Accordingly, one should inquire into things carefully. It is the same for martial training as for official business.

When one attempts to concentrate things in this manner, won't daily negligence and today's lack of resolve be understood?

Even though one has made some blunder in governmental work, it can probably be excused by pleading clumsiness or inexperience. But what kind of excuse may be given for the failure of the men who were involved in this recent unexpected event?" Master Jin'emon always used to say, "It is enough if a warrior is simply a stalwart," and this is just such a case. If one felt that such a failure were a mortification, it would be the least he could do to cut open his stomach, rather than live on in shame with a burning in his breast and the feeling that he had no place to go, and, as his luck as a warrior had run out, he was no longer able to function quickly and had been given a bad name. But if one regretted losing his life and reasoned that he should live because such a death would be useless, then for the next five, ten or twenty years of his life, he would be pointed at from behind and covered with shame. After his death his corpse would be smeared with disgrace, his guiltless descendants would receive his dishonor for having been born in his line, his ancestors' name would be dragged down, and all the members of his family would be blemished. Such circumstances are truly regrettable.

If one has no earnest daily intention, does not consider what it is to be a warrior even in his dreams, and lives through the day idly, he can be said to be worthy of punishment.

Presumably it can be said that a man who has been cut down was lacking in ability and had run out of luck as a warrior. The man who cut him down, compelled by unavoidable circumstances and feeling that there was nothing else to be done, also put his life on the line, and thus there should be no evidence of cowardice. Being short-tempered is inappropriate, but it cannot be said that two men who face each other are cowards. In this recent event, however, the men who lived and covered themselves with shame were not true warriors.

One should every day think over and make an effort to implant in his mind the saying, "At that time is right now." It is said that it is strange indeed that anyone is able to pass through life by one means or another in negligence. Thus, the Way of the Samurai is, morning after morning, the practice of death, considering whether it will be here or be there, imagining the most slightly way of dying, and putting one's mind firmly in death. Although this may be a most difficult thing, if one will do it, it can be done. There is nothing that one should suppose cannot be done.

Moreover, the influence of words is important in military affairs. It would have been best for stopping the man in this recent event, too.

When the situation is too much, one may either cut the man down, or, if the man is escaping, yell something like, "Don't run ! Only cowards run !" and thus, according to what the situation demands, achieve one's goals by the influence of words. There was a certain man who was said to be good at judging men's dispositions and formerly had everyone's attention, and he was able to handle such cases. This is proof that "right now" is no different from "when the time comes." The position of yokoza no yari is another example of this.* It is something that should be made one's aim beforehand.

The things to be deeply considered beforehand are many. If there is someone who has killed a man in the lord's mansion and has managed to escape, as one does not know whether he may still be swinging his sword and advancing toward the room next to the lord's, he should cut the man down. Indeed, one may be blamed later in an investigation as a confederate of the killer, or as someone who had a grudge against him. But at that time one should think only of cutting the man down and not anticipate later blame.

Even if one's head were to be suddenly cut off, he should be able to do one more action with certainty. The last moments of Nitta Yoshisada are proof of this. Had his spirit been weak, he would have fallen the moment his head was severed. Recently, there is the example of Ono Doken. These actions occurred because of simple determination. With martial valor, if one becomes like a revengeful ghost and shows great determination, though his head is cut off, he should not die.

Whether people be of high or low birth, rich or poor, old or young, enlightened or confused, they are all alike in that they will one day die. It is not that we don't know that we are going to die, but we grasp at straws. While knowing that we will die someday, we think that all the others will die before us and that we will be the last to go. Death seems a long way off.

Is this not shallow thinking? It is worthless and is only a joke within a dream. It will not do to think in such a way and be negligent. Insofar as death is always at one's door, one should make sufficient effort and act quickly.

It is good to carry some powdered rouge in one's sleeve. It may happen that when one is sobering up or waking from sleep, his complexion may be poor. At such a time it is good to take out and apply some powdered rouge.

There are times when a person gets carried away and talks on without thinking much. But this can be seen by observers when one's mind is flippant and lacking truth. After such an occasion it is best to come face to face with the truth and express it. The truth will then be arrived at in one's own heart too. Even when greeting someone lightly, one should consider the circumstances and after deliberation speak in a way that will not injure the man's feelings.

Furthermore, if there is a person who is criticizing the Way of the Samurai or one's own province, one should speak with him severely, without the least bit of ceremony. One must be resolved in advance.

Although a person who excels in an art regards others as competitors, last year Hyodo Sachu gave up the title of Master of Renga to Yamaguchi Shochin. A praiseworthy act.

The priest Tannen used to hang up wind-bells but said, "It's not because I like the sound. I hang them in order to know the wind conditions in the event of fire, for that is the only worry in having a large temple." When the wind blew, he himself walked about at night. Throughout his whole life the fire in his brazier was never out, and he always put a paper lantern and lighter by his pillow. He said, ' 'People are flustered during an emergency, and there is no one to quickly strike a light."

If one makes a distinction between public places and one's sleeping quarters, or between being on the battlefield and on the tatami, when the moment comes there will not be time for making amends. There is only the matter of constant awareness. If it were not for men who demonstrate valor on the tatami, one could not find them on the battlefield either.

Bravery and cowardice are not things that can be conjectured in times of peace. They are in different categories.

Though it may be said that the gods dislike impurity, if one thinks a bit, he will see that he has not been negligent in his daily worship. Thus, one's previous faithfulness has been exactly for the sake of praying for good fortune in such times as when one is barbed in blood and climbing over the dead. At such a time, if it is a god that turns back when one is defiled, then one should know clearly that praying is ineffective and should worship regardless of defilement.

At times of great trouble or disaster, one word will suffice. At times of happiness, too, one word will be enough. And when meeting or talking with others, one word will do. One should think well and then speak. This is clear and firm, and one should learn it with no doubts. It is a matter of putting forth one's whole effort and having the correct attitude previously. This is very difficult to explain but is something that everyone should work on in his heart. If a person has not learned this in his heart, it is not likely that he will understand it.

Human life is truly a short affair. It is better to live doing the things that you like. It is foolish to live within this dream of a world seeing unpleasantness and doing only things that you do not like. But it is important never to tell this to young people as it is something that would be harmful if incorrectly understood.

Personally, I like to sleep. And I intend to appropriately confine myself more and more to my living quarters and pass my life away sleeping.

I had a dream on the night of the twenty-eighth day of the twelfth month in the third year of Shotoku. The content of the dream changed gradually to the extent that I strengthened my will. The condition of a person is revealed by his dreams. It would be good to make companions of your dreams and to put forth effort.

Shame and repentance are like upsetting a pot of water. When a certain friend of mine listened to the way that a man who had stolen his sword ornament confessed, he felt compassion. If one will rectify his mistakes, their traces will soon disappear.

According to what the Buddhist priest Kaion said, a person becomes more and more prideful if he gains a little understanding because he thinks he knows his own limits and weak points. However, it is a difficult thing to truly know one's own limits and weak points.

At a glance, every individual's own measure of dignity is manifested just as it is. There is dignity in personal appearance. There is dignity in a calm aspect. There is dignity in a paucity of words. There is dignity in flawlessness of manners. There is dignity in solemn behavior. And there is dignity in deep insight and a clear perspective.

These are all reflected on the surface. But in the end, their foundation is simplicity of thought and tautness of spirit.

Covetousness, anger and foolishness are things to sort out well. When bad things happen in the world, if you look at them comparatively, they are not unrelated to these three things. Looking comparatively at the good things, you will see that they are not excluded from wisdom, humanity and bravery.

This is according to what Nakano Kazuma Toshiaki said. There are people who feel that using old utensils for the Tea Ceremony is coarse, and that it is better to use new, clean utensils. There are also people who are wont to use old materials because of their lack of gaudiness. Both are mistaken. Old utensils, although they are things that are used by the humble, are also used by the higher classes because of their value. Their value is revered.

A retainer is just like this. A person rises from the humble to the higher classes because he has value. At the same time, to feel that a person of no family cannot do the same work as one of higher family, or that a man who has heretofore been only a foot soldier should not be allowed to become a leader, is entirely wrong thinking. As for a person who has risen from the humble, his value should be prized and especially respected, even more than that of a person who was born into his class.

My father Jin'emon said that when he was young he was taken from time to time to the entrance of the Chinese settlement in order to be exposed to the atmosphere of the city and to become used to people. From the time he was five years old he was sent as family representative to various people's homes, and in order to make him strong he was made to put on a warrior's straw sandals and visit the temples of his ancestors from the time he was seven.

It is said that one will not be able to do great works if he does not behave with some reserve towards his master, the chief retainers and elders. What is done casually and freely will not work out well. It is a matter of attitude.

It is unfitting that one be ignorant of the history and origins of his clan and its retainers. But there are times when extensive knowledge becomes a hindrance. One should use discretion. Knowing the circumstances can be an obstruction in everyday affairs, too. One should use discretion.

It is written that the priest Shungaku said, "In just refusing to retreat from something one gains the strength of two men." This is interesting. Something that is not done at that time and at that place will remain unfinished for a lifetime. At a time when it is difficult to complete matters with the strength of a single man, one will bring it to a conclusion with the strength of two. If one thinks about it later, he will be negligent all his life.

"Stamp quickly and pass through a wall of iron" is another interesting phrase. To quickly break in and stamp through directly is the first step of celerity. In connection with this, Hideyoshi can be thought of as the only man who has grasped solidly the chance of a lifetime since the creation of Japan.

People who talk on and on about matters of little importance probably have some complaint in the back of their mind. But in order to be ambiguous and to hide this they repeat what they are saving over and over. To hear something like this causes doubt to arise in one's breast.

One should be careful and not say things that are likely to cause trouble at the time. When some difficulty arises in this world, people get excited, and before one knows it the matter is on everyone's lips. This is useless. If worse comes to worse, you may become the subject of gossip, or at least you will have made enemies by saying something unnecessary and will have created ill will. It is said that at such a time it is better to stay at home and think of poetry.

To talk about other people's affairs is a great mistake. To praise them, too, is unfitting. In any event, it is best to know your own ability well, to put forth effort in your endeavors, and to be discreet in speech.

The heart of a virtuous person has settled down and he does not rush about at things. A person of little merit is not at peace but walks about making trouble and is in conflict with all.

It is a good viewpoint to see the world as a dream. When you have something like a nightmare, you will wake up and tell yourself that it was only a dream. It is said that the world we live in is not a bit different from this.

People with intelligence will use it to fashion things both true and false and will try to push through whatever they want with their clever reasoning. This is injury from intelligence. Nothing you do will have effect if you do not use truth.

In affairs like law suits or even in arguments, by losing quickly one will lose in fine fashion. It is like sumo [wrestling]. If one thinks only of winning, a sordid victory will be worse than a defeat. For the most part, it becomes a squalid defeat.

Feeling deeply the difference between oneself and others, bearing ill will and falling out with people-these things come from a heart that lacks compassion. If one wraps up everything with a heart of compassion, there will be no coming into conflict with people.

A person who knows but a little will put on an air of knowledge. This is a matter of inexperience. When someone knows something well, it will not be seen in his manner. This person is genteel.

When going someplace for a talk or something similar, it is best to let the person know ahead of time, and then go. To go without knowing whether the other party is busy, or when he has some particular anxiety, is awkward. There is nothing that surpasses not going where you have not been invited. Good friends are rare. Even if someone is invited somewhere, he should use understanding. It is difficult to feel deeply the sensitivities of people other than those who go out only rarely. Fiascos at pleasure gatherings are numerous.

However, you should not be brusque towards a person who has come to visit, even if you are busy.

It is bad to carry even a good thing too far. Even concerning things such as Buddhism, Buddhist sermons, and moral lessons, talking too much will bring harm.

The late Jin'emon said that it is better not to bring up daughters. They are a blemish to the family name and a shame to the parents. The eldest daughter is special, but it is better to disregard the others.

The priest Keiho related that Lord Aki once said that martial valor is a matter of becoming a fanatic. I thought that this was surprisingly in accord with my own resolve and thereafter became more and more extreme in my fanaticism.

The late Nakano Kazuma said that the original purpose of the Tea Ceremony is to cleanse the six senses. For the eyes there are the hanging scroll and flower arrangement. For the nose there is the incense. For the ears there is the sound of the hot water. For the mouth there is the taste of the tea. And for the hands and feet there is the correctness of term. When the five senses have thus been cleansed, the mind will of itself be purified. The Tea Ceremony will cleanse the mind when the mind is clogged up. I do not depart from the heart of the Tea Ceremony for twenty-four hours a day, yet this is absolutely not a matter of tasteful living. Moreover, the tea utensils are something that should be in accord with one's social position.

In the poem, "Under the deep snows in the last village/ Last night numerous branches of plum blossomed," the opulence of the phrase "numerous branches" was changed to "a single branch." It is said that this "single branch" contains true tranquility.

When intimate friends, allies, or people who are indebted to you have done some wrong, you should secretly reprimand them and intervene between them and society in a good manner. You should erase a person's bad reputation and praise him as a matchless ally and one man in a thousand. If you wilt thus reprimand a person in private and with good understanding, his blemish will heal and he will become good. If you praise a person, people's hearts will change and an ill reputation will go away of itself. It is important to have the single purpose of handling all things with compassion and doing things well. A certain person said the following.

There are two kinds of dispositions, inward and outward, and a person who is lacking in one or the other is worthless. It is, for example, like the blade of a sword, which one should sharpen well and then put in its scabbard, periodically taking it out and knitting one's eyebrows as in an attack, wiping of the blade, and then placing it in its scabbard again.

If a person has his sword out all the time, he is habitually swinging a naked blade; people will not approach him and he will have no allies.

If a sword is always sheathed, it will become rusty, the blade will dull, and people will think as much of its owner.

One cannot accomplish things simply with cleverness. One must take a broad view. It will not do to make rash judgments concerning good and evil. However, one should not be sluggish. It is said that one is not truly a samurai if he does not make his decisions quickly and break right through to completion.

Once, when a group of five or six pages were traveling to the capital together in the same boat, it happened that their boat struck a regular ship late at night. Five or six seamen from the ship leapt aboard and loudly demanded that the pages give up their boat's anchor, in accord with the seaman's code. Hearing this, the pages ran forward yelling, "The seaman's code is something for people like you! Do you think that we samurai are going to let you take equipment from a boat carrying warriors? We will cut you down and throw you into the sea to the last man!" With that, all the seamen fled back to their own ship.

At such a time, one must act like a samurai. For trifling occasions it is better to accomplish things simply by yelling. By making something more significant than it really is and missing one's chance, an affair will not be brought to a close and will be no accomplishment at all.

A certain person who came up with a cash shortage when closing out an account book sent a letter to his section leader saying, "It is regrettable to have to commit seppuku over a matter of money. As you are my section leader, please send some funds." Since this was reasonable, the balance was provided and the matter was closed. It is said that even wrongdoings can be managed without detection.

By being impatient, matters are damaged and great works cannot be done. If one considers something not to be a matter of time, it will be done surprisingly quickly. Times change. Think about the world fifteen years from now. It should be rather different, but if one were to look into a book of prophecies, I imagine that it would not be that different. In the passing fifteen years, not one of the useful men of today will be left. And even if men who are young now come forth, probably less than half will make it. Worth gradually wanes. For example, if there were a shortage of gold, silver would become treasure, and if there were a shortage of silver, copper would be valued. With changing times and the waning of men's capacities, one would be of suitable worth even if he put forth only slight effort. Something like fifteen years is the space of a dream. If a man but takes care of his health, in the end he will have accomplished his purpose and will be a valuable person. Certainly in a period when masters are many, one must put forth considerable effort. But at the time when the world is sliding into a decline, to excel is easy.

To put forth great effort in correcting a person's bad habits is the way it should be done. One should be like the digger wasp. It is said that even with an adopted child, if you teach him continually so that he will resemble you, he surely will.

If your strength is only that which comes from vitality, your words and personal conduct will appear to be in accord with the Way, and you will be praised by others. But when you question yourself about this, there will be nothing to be said. The last line of the poem that goes, "When your own heart asks," is the secret principle of all the arts. It is said that it is a good censor.

When you are listening to the stories of accomplished men and the like, you should listen with deep sincerity, even if it's something about which you already know. If in listening to the same thing ten or twenty times it happens that you come to an unexpected understanding, that moment will be very special. Within the tedious talk of old folks are their meritorious deeds.

CHAPTER 3

Lord Naoshige once said

Lord Naoshige once said, "There is nothing felt quite so deeply as giri. There are times when someone like a cousin dies and it is not a matter of shedding tears. But we may hear of someone who lived fifty or a hundred years ago, of whom we know nothing and who has no family ties with us whatsoever, and yet from a sense giri shed tears."

When Lord Naoshige was passing by a place called Chiriku, someone said to him, ' 'In this place there lives a man who is over ninety years old. Since this man is so fortunate, why don't you stop and see him?" Naoshige heard this and said, "How could anyone be more pitiful than this man? How many of his children and grandchildren do you suppose he has seen fall before his very eyes? Where is the good fortune in that?"

It seems that he did not stop to see the man.

When Lord Naoshige was speaking to his grandson, Lord Motoshige, he said, "No matter whether one be of high or low rank, a family line is something that will decline when it's time has come. If one tries to keep it from going to ruin at that time, it will have an unsightly finish. If one thinks that the time has come, it is best to let it go down with good grace. Doing so, he may even cause it to be maintained."

It is said that Motoshige's younger brother heard this from him.

CHAPTER 4

When Nabeshima Tadanao

WHEN Nabeshima Tadanao was fifteen years old, a manservant in the kitchen committed some rude act and a foot soldier was about to beat him, but in the end the servant cut the soldier down.

The clan elders deemed the death sentence appropriate, saying that the man had in the first place erred in matters concerning the ranks of men, and that he had also shed the blood of his opponent. Tadanao heard this and said, "Which is worse, to err in matters concerning the ranks of men or to stray from the Way of the Samurai ?"

The elders were unable to answer. Then Tadanao said, "I have read that when the crime itself is unclear, the punishment should be light. Put him in confinement for a while."

Once, when Lord Katsushige was hunting at Shiroishi, he shot a large boar. Everyone came running up to see it and said, "Well, well. You have brought down an uncommonly large one !" Suddenly the boar got up and dashed into their midst. All of them fled in confusion, but Nabeshima Matabet drew his sword and finished it off. At that point Lord Katsushige covered his face with his sleeve and said, "It sure is dusty." This was presumably because he did not want to see the spectacle of his flustered men.

When Lord Katsushige was young, he was instructed by his father, Lord Naoshige, "For practice in cutting, execute some men who have been condemned to death." Thus, in the place that is now within the western gate, ten men were lined up, and Katsushige continued to decapitate one after another until he had executed nine of them. When he came to the tenth, he saw that the man was young and healthy and said, "I'm tired of cutting now. I'll spare this man's life." And the man's life was saved.

Lord Katsushige always used to say that there are four kinds of retainers. They are the "quick, then lapping," the "lagging, then quick," the "continually quick," and the "continually lagging."

The "continually quick" are men who when given orders will undertake their execution quickly and settle the matter well. Fukuchi Kichizaemon and the like resemble this type.

The "lagging, then quick" are men who, though lacking in understanding when given orders, prepare quickly and bring the matter to a conclusion. I suppose that Nakano Kazuma and men similar are like this.

The "quick, then lagging" are men who when given orders seem to be going to settle things but in their preparation take time and procrastinate. There are many people like this.

Other than these, one could say that the rest are "continually lagging."

CHAPTER 6

When Lord Takanobu

WHEN Lord Takanobu was at the Battle of Bungo, a messenger came from the enemy camp bearing sake and food. Takanobu wanted to partake of this quickly, but the men at his side stopped him, saying,

"Presents from the enemy are likely to be poisoned. This is not something that a general should eat."

Takanobu heard them out and then said, "Even if it is poisoned, how much of an effect would that have on things? Call the messenger here!" He then broke open the barrel right in front of the messenger, drank three large cups of sake, offered the messenger one too, gave him a reply, and sent him back to his camp.

Takagi Akifusa turned against the Ryuzoji clan, appealed to Maeda Iyo no kami Iesada, and was sheltered by him. Akifusa was a warrior of matchless valor and was an accomplished and agile swordsman. His retainers were Ingazaemon and Fudozaemon, stalwarts in no way inferior, and they left Akifusa's side neither day nor night. Thus it happened that a request was sent from Lord Takanobu to Iesada to kill Akifusa. At one point, when Akifusa was seated on the veranda having Ingazaemon wash his feet, Iesada came running up behind him and struck off his head, Before his head fell, Akifusa drew out his short sword and turned to strike, but cut off Ingazaemon's head. The two heads fell into the wash basin together. Akifusa's head then rose into the midst of those present. This was the sort of magic technique that he consistently had.

The priest Tannen used to say in his daily talks that: A monk cannot fulfill the Buddhist Way if he does not manifest compassion without and persistently store up courage within. And if a warrior does not manifest courage on the outside and hold enough compassion within his heart to burst his chest, he cannot become a retainer. Therefore, the monk pursues courage with the warrior as his model, and the warrior pursues the compassion of the monk.

I traveled about for many years and met men of wisdom but never found the means to the pursuit of knowledge. Therefore, whenever I heard of a man of courage in one place or another, I would go and look for him regardless of the hardships on the way. I have learned clearly that these stories of the Way of the Samurai have been an aid on the road to Buddhism. Now a warrior with his armor will rush into the enemy camp, making that armor his strength. Do you suppose that a monk with a single rosary can dash into the midst of spears and long swords, armed with only meekness and compassion? If he does not have great courage, he will do no dashing at all. As proof of this, the priest offering the incense at a great Buddhist memorial service may tremble, and this is because he has no courage.

Things like kicking a man back from the dead, or pulling all living creatures out of hell, are all matters of courage. Nevertheless, monks of recent times all entertain false ideas and desire to become laudably gentle; there are none who complete the Way. Furthermore, among warriors there are some cowards who advance Buddhism. These are regrettable matters. It is a great mistake for a young samurai to learn about Buddhism. The reason is that he will see things in two ways. A person who does not set himself in just one direction will be of no value at all. It is fine for retired old men to learn about Buddhism as a diversion, but if a warrior makes loyalty and filial piety one load, and courage and compassion another, and carries these twenty-four hours a day until his shoulders wear out, he will be a samurai.

In one's morning and evening worship, and as one goes about his day, he had best recite the name of his master. It is not a bit different from the Buddha's names and holy words. Furthermore, one should be in harmony with his family gods. These are matters of the strength of one's fate. Compassion is like a mother who nurtures one's fate. Examples of the ruin of merciless warriors who were brave alone are conspicuous in both past and present.

There was a certain point in the conversation when a retainer of Lord Nabeshima Naohiro said, "There are no men here upon whom the master can truly rely. Although I am consistently useless, I am the only one who would throw away his life for you."

It is said that Lord Naohiro got outrageously angry, saying, "Among our retainers there is not a one who holds his life in regret! You are talking arrogance!" and he was at the point of striking him when the man was pulled away by others who were there.

Once when Master Tanesada, the founder of the China family, was coming by sea to the island of Shikoku, a strong wind began blowing and the boat was damaged. The boat was saved from sinking by abalone gathering together and covering over the damaged sections. From that time on none of the China family nor any of its retainers ate abalone. If one of them mistakenly ate one, it is said that his body was covered with boils in the shape of abalone.

At the fall of the castle at Arima, on the twenty-eighth day in the vicinity of the inmost citadel, Mitsuse Gender sat down on a levee between the fields. When Nakano Shintohi passed by and asked the reason for this, Mitsuse replied, "I have abdominal pains and can't go a step farther. I have sent the members of my group ahead, so please take command." This situation was reported by the overseer, pronounced to be a case of cowardice, and Mitsuse was ordered to commit seppuku.

Long ago, abdominal pains were called "cowardice grass." This is because they come suddenly and render a person immobile.

At the time of Lord Nabeshima Naohiro's death, Lord Mitsushige forbade Naohiro's retainers the practice of tsuifuku. His messenger went to Naohiro's mansion and made the declaration, but those who received this news could in no way agree to it. From their midst Ishimaru Uneme (later called Seizaemon) spoke from the lowest seat, "It is improper for me as a younger person to speak out, but I think that what Lord Katsushige has said is reasonable. As a person who received the master's care when I was young, I had whole heartedly decided on tsuifuku. But hearing Lord Katsushige's dictum and being convinced of his reasoning, no matter what the others may do, I am giving up the idea of tsuifuku and will serve the master's successor." Hearing this, the others all followed suit.

Once Lord Masaie was playing shogi with Lord Hideyoshi and there were a number of daimyo watching. When it came time to withdraw, although Lord Masaie could stand, his feet were numb and he could not walk. He made his withdrawal crawling away, causing everyone to laugh. Because Lord Masaie was big and obese he was not ordinarily able to be on his knees. After this event he thought it would not be fitting to be in attendance anymore and began refusing such duties.

Nakano Uemonnosuke Tadaaki was killed on the twelfth day of the eighth month in the sixth year of Eiroku, at the time of the fight between Master Goto and Master Hirai of Suko on the island of Kabashima in the Kishima district. When Uemonnosuke was leaving for the front lines, he embraced his son Shikibu (later called Jin'emon) in the garden and, although Shikibu was very young, said, "When you grow up, win honor in the Way of the Samurai!"

Even when the children in his family were very young, Yamamoto Jin'emon would draw near to them and say, "Grow up to be a great stalwart, and be of good use to your master." He said, "It is good to breathe these things into their ears even when they are too young to understand."

When Ogawa Toshikiyo's legitimate son Sahei Kiyoji died as a youth, there was one young retainer who galloped up to the temple and committed seppuku.

When Taku Nagato no kami Yasuyori passed away, Kola Yataemon said that he had been unable to repay the master's kindness and committed seppuku.

CHAPTER 7

Narutomi Hyogo said

NARUTOMI HYOGO said, "What is called winning is defeating one's allies. Defeating one's allies is defeating oneself, and defeating oneself is vigorously overcoming one's own body. "

It is as though a man were in the midst of ten thousand allies but not a one were following him. If one hasn't previously mastered his mind and body, he will not defeat the enemy." During the Shimabara Rebellion, his armor being still at the encampment, Shugyo Echizen no kami Tanenao participated in the fight dressed only in hakama and haori. It is said that he died in battle in this attire.

At the time of the attack on the castle at Shimabara, Tazaki Geki was wearing very resplendent armor. Lord Katsushige was not pleased by this, and after that every time he saw something showy he would say, "That's just like Geki's armor."

In the light of this story, military armor and equipment that are showy can be seen as being weak and having no strength. By them one can see through the wearer's heart.

When Nabeshima wizen no kami Tadanao died, his attendant Ezoe Kinbei took his remains and had them consecrated at Mt. Kola. Then, confining himself in a hermitage, he carved a statue of his master and another of himself doing reverence before the master. On the first anniversary of Tadanao's death, he returned to his home and committed tsuifuku. Later the statue was taken from Mt. Koya and was placed at the Kodenji.

In the generation of Lord Mitsushige, Oishi Kosuke was at first a foot soldier serving at the side of his master. Whenever Lord Mitsushige was making the trip for his alternate year residence in Edo, Kosuke would make the rounds around the sleeping quarters of his master, and if he thought a certain area to be insecure, he would spread a straw mat and pass through the night awake by himself. In rainy weather he would simply wear a bamboo hat and an oilpaper raincoat and would stand watch while being pelted by the rain. It is said that to the end he never spent a single night in negligence.

When Oishi Kosuke was an uchitonin, a mysterious person sneaked into the area of the maids' chambers late at night.' There was a great commotion from upstairs to down and men and women of all ranks were running about; only Kosuke was not to be seen. While the senior ladies-in-waiting were searching about, Kosuke yanked his sword from its scabbard and waited quietly in the room next to the master's bedchamber. As all was in confusion, he had felt apprehension for the master and was there to protect him. Because of this it was said that his viewpoint was quite different.

The man who had sneaked in was Narutomi Kichibei. He and his accomplice Hamada Ichizaemon were condemned to death for adultery.

Once when Lord Katsushige was hunting at Nishime, for some reason he got very angry. He drew his sword from his obi, scabbard and all, and began beating Soejima Zennojo with it, but his hand slipped and his sword fell into a ravine. Zennojo, in order to stay with the sword, fumbled down into the ravine and picked it up. This done, he stuck the sword in his lapel, crawled up the precipice, and just as he was, offered the sword to his master. In terms of quick-mindedness and reserve this was matchless resource.

Once when Master Sane Ukyo was crossing over the Takao River, the bridge was being repaired and there was one large piling that could not be pulled up. Master Ukyo dismounted, grasped the piling firmly, pave a shout, and began to pull it up. There was a tremendous sound, and although he was able to pull it up to his own height, it would go no further and thereupon sank. After he returned home he became sick and suddenly died.

At the time of the funeral at the temple in Jobaru, when the funeral procession crossed the Takao Bridge, the corpse leapt from the casket and fell into the river. A sixteen-year-old acolyte from the Shufukuji immediately jumped into the river and took hold of the dead body. Everyone then ran down into the river and pulled up the corpse. The head monk was very impressed and instructed the other acolytes to be guided by this young man. It is said that he later became a very famous monk.

Yamamoto Kichizaemon was ordered by his father Jin'emon to cut down a dog at the age of five, and at the age of fifteen he was made to execute a criminal. Everyone, by the time they were fourteen or fifteen, was ordered to do a beheading without fail. When Lord Katsushige was young, he was ordered by Lord Naoshige to practice killing with a sword. It is said that at that time he was made to cut down more than ten men successively.

A long time ago this practice was followed, especially in the upper classes, but today even the children of the lower classes perform no executions, and this is extreme negligence. To say that one can do without this sort of thing, or that there is no merit in killing a condemned man, or that it is a crime, or that it is defiling, is to make excuses. In short, can it not be thought that because a person's martial valor is weak, his attitude is only that of trimming his nails and being attractive?

If one investigates into the spirit of a man who finds these things disagreeable, one sees that this person gives himself over to cleverness and excuse making not to kill because he feels unnerved. But Naoshige made it his orders exactly because this is something that must be done.

Last year I went to the Kase Execution Grounds to try my hand at beheading, and I found it to be an extremely good feeling. To think that it is unnerving is a symptom of cowardice.

Among the pageboys in forelocks in Lord Mitsushige's retinue, one Tomoda Shozaemon was in attendance. A rather wanton fellow, he fell in love with a leading actor of the theater by the name of Tamon Shozaemon and changed both his name and his crest to that of the actor. Completely abandoning himself to this affair, he spent everything he had and lost all his clothing and furnishings. And at length, when he had exhausted all his means, he stole Mawatari Rokubei's sword and had a spearman take it to a pawnshop.

The spearman, however, spoke up about this matter, and in the investigation both he and Shozaemon were condemned to death. The investigator was Yamamoto Gorozaemon. When he read the report, he spoke in a loud voice and said, "The man who accuses the defendant is Spearman so-and-so."

Mitsushige responded quickly, "Put him to death."

When it came time to announce his fate to Shozaemon, Gorozaemon came in and said, "There is now nothing left to be done for you. Prepare yourself for your place of death."

Shozaemon settled himself and said, "Very well. I understand what you have said and am grateful for your words." Due to somebody's trickery, however, while a kaishaku was introduced to Shozaemon, it was arranged that a foot soldier, Naozuka Rokuuemon, was to step from the side and decapitate him.

Repairing to the execution grounds, where the kaishaku stood opposite him, Shozaemon saluted him with extreme calm. But just then, seeing Naozuka drawing his sword, he jumped up and said, "Who are you? I'll never let you cut off my head!" From that point on his peace of mind was shattered and he showed terrible cowardice. Finally he was brought to the ground, stretched out, and decapitated.

Gorozaemon later said secretly, ' 'If he hadn't been deceived, he would have probably met his death well."

Noda Kizaemon said about the function of kaishaku, "When a man who has come to his place of death loses his wits and is crawling about, it is likely seine damage will be done when it comes time to perform kaishak. At such a time first wait a bit and by some means gather your strength. Then if you cut by standing firm and not missing the chance, you will do well."

In the generation of Lord Katsushige there were retainers who, regardless of high or low rank, were requested to work before the master from the time they were young. When Shiba Kizaemon was doing such service, once the master was clipping his nails and said, "Throw these away." Kizaemon held them in his hand but did not stand up, and the master said, "What's the matter?" Kizaemon said, "There's one missing." The master said, ' 'Here it is," and banded over the one that he had hidden.

Sawabe Heizaemon was ordered to commit seppuku on the eleventh day of the eleventh month in the second year of Tenna. As this became known to him on the night of the tenth, he sent a request to Yamamoto Gonnojo [Tsunetomo] to be kaishaku. The following is a copy of Yamamoto's reply. (Tsunetomo was twenty-four years old at this time.)

I am in accord with your resolution and accept your request for me to function as kaishaku. I instinctively felt that I should decline, but as this is to take place tomorrow there is no time for making excuses and I will undertake the job. The fact that you have chosen me from among many people is a great personal satisfaction to me. Please set your mind at ease concerning all that must follow. Although it is now late at night, I will come to your house to talk over the particulars.

When Heizaemon saw this reply, it is said that he remarked, "This is a matchless letter."

From ages past it has been considered ill-omened by samurai to be requested as kaishaku. The reason for this is that one pains no fame even if the job is well done. And if by chance one should blunder, it becomes a lifetime disgrace.

Once when Tanaka Yahei was attending to affairs in Edo, one of his menials was rather insolent and Yahei scolded him severely. Late that night Yahei heard the noise of someone coming up the stairs. He felt this to be suspicious and quietly got up. With short sword in hand he asked who was there, and it turned out to be the menial whom he had scolded previously, secretly holding a short sword. Yahei leapt down and with a single stroke cut the man down. I heard many people later state that he had had good luck.

A certain Master Tokuhisa was born quite different from other people and looked to be a bit moronic. Once, a guest was invited and mudfish salad was served. At that time everyone said, "Master Tokuhisa's mudfish salad," and laughed. Later when he was in attendance and a certain person made fun of him by quoting the above remark, Tokuhisa pulled out his sword and cut the man down. This event was investigated and it was stated to Lord Naoshige, "Seppuku is recommended because this was a matter of rashness within the palace."

When Lord Naoshige heard this, he said, ' 'To be made fun of and remain silent is cowardice. There is no reason to overlook this fact because one is within the palace. A man who makes fun of people is himself a fool. It was his own fault for being cut down."

Once when Nakano Mokunosuke boarded a small boat on the Sumida River to enjoy the coolness, a rogue got in too and committed all manner of rude acts. When Mokunosuke saw that the rogue was relieving himself over the side of the boat, he cut the man's head off and it fell into the river. So that people would not notice this, he quickly covered the body with various things. He then said to the boatman, "This matter should not become known. Row up to the upper reaches of the river and bury the corpse. I shall naturally pay you well."

The boatman did as he was told, but in the lagoon where the body was buried Mokunosuke cut off the head of the boatman and returned directly. It is said that this fact never became known publicly. At that time there was also one young homosexual male prostitute riding in the boat. Mekunosuke said, "That fellow was a man too. It is best to learn how to cut a man while one is still young," and so the man cut the corpse once. Because of that the young man said nothing later on.

It is said that every time Oki Hyobu's group gathered and after all their affairs were finished he would say, "Young men should discipline themselves rigorously in intention and courage. This will be accomplished if only courage is fixed in one's heart. If one's sword is broken, he will strike with his hands. If his hands are cut off, he will press the enemy down with his shoulders. If his shoulders are cut away, he will bite through ten or fifteen enemy necks with his teeth. Courage is such a thing."

Shida Kichinosuke said, "At first it is an oppressive thing to run until one is breathless. But it is an extraordinarily good feeling when one is standing around after the running. More than that, it is even better to sit down. More than that, it is even better to lie down. And more than that, to put down a pillow and sleep soundly is even better. A man's whole life should be like this. To exert oneself to a great extent when one is young and then to sleep when he is old or at the point of death is the way it should be. But to first sleep and then exert oneself.. . To exert oneself to the end, and to end one's whole life in toil is regrettable." Shimomura Rokurouemon told this story.

A saying of Kichinosuke's that is similar to this is, "A man's life should be as toilsome as possible."

When Ueno Rihei was overseer of accounting in Edo, he had a young assistant whom he treated in a very intimate way. On the first night of the eighth month he went drinking with Hashimoto Taemon, an overseer of foot soldiers, and got so drunk that he lost good sense. He accompanied his young assistant back home, babbling on in a drunken manner, and when they arrived there, Rihei said that he was going to cut the assistant down. The assistant pushed away the tip of Rihei's scabbard. They grappled and both fell into the gutter with the assistant on top pushing Rihei down. At this time, Rihei's servant ran up and asked, "Is Master Rihei on the top or on the bottom?"

When Rihei replied, "I'm on the bottom !" the servant stabbed the assistant once. The assistant got up and, as his wound was light, ran away.

When the affair was brought under investigation, Rihei was put into confinement at the Naekiyama prison and was condemned to capital punishment by beheading. Before this, when he was positioned in Edo and living in a rented house in the merchants' district, a servant had opposed him and he had cut him down. But he had acted in a good way at that time, and people said that he had acted like a man. This time, however, his actions were outrageous and were certainly unnecessary.

If one thinks about this well from beginning to end, to get so drunk as to draw one's sword is both cowardice and lack of resolve. Rihei's servant was a man from Taku, but his name is not remembered. Though he was a member of the lower classes, he was a brave man. It is said that Taemon committed suicide during the investigation.

In the twelfth section of the fifth chapter of the Ryoankyo there is this story:

In the Province of Wizen there was a certain man from Take who, although he had contracted smallpox, was considering joining the forces attacking the castle at Shimabara. His parents earnestly tried to get him to desist, saying, "With such a grave illness, even if you should get there, how could you be of any use?"

He replied, "It would be to my satisfaction to die on the way. After having received the warm benevolence of the master, should I tell myself that I will be of no use to him now?" And he left for the front. Although it was winter camp and the cold was extreme, he did not pay any attention to his health, and neither put on many layers of clothing nor took off his armor day or night. Moreover, he did not avoid uncleanliness, and in the end recovered quickly and was able to fulfill his loyalty completely. So to the contrary of what you would expect, it cannot be said that one is to despise uncleanliness.

When the teacher, Suzuki Shozo, heard this, he said, "Was it not a cleansing act to throw away his life for his master? For a man who will cut of his life for the sake of righteousness, there is no need to call upon the god of smallpox. All the gods of heaven will protect him. " Lord Katsushige said, "Whether a man of Hizen holds death in regret or not is not a matter of concern. What I worry about is that people will not take to heart the command to keep the rules of manners and etiquette correctly. I am afraid that the entire clan, our relatives and elders, out of too much earnestness, will feel that the command to keep correct etiquette is an exaggeration. Up to now there have existed men who were used to these things, and even if etiquette was slightly wrong, they could remember the correct way, and the matter was settled. I have given this command because people are negligent in affairs of this sort."

During the Genroku period there was a samurai of low rank from the Province of Ise by the name of Suzuki Rokubei. He was ill with a severe fever, and his consciousness became dim. At that time a certain male nurse was unexpectedly stricken with greed and was about to open up the ink box and steal the money that was kept in it. Just then the sick man suddenly stirred, took the sword from the base of his pillow, and in a sudden attack cut the man down with one blow. With that, the sick man fell back and died. By this act, Rokubei seemed to be a man of principled disposition.

I heard this story in Edo, but later when I was serving in the same province with a Dr. Nagatsuka, who was also from the Province of Ise, I asked him about it, and indeed he knew the story and said that it was true.

CHAPTER 8

On the night of the thirteenth day

ON THE NIGHT of the thirteenth day of the ninth month in the fourth year of Teikyo, there was a group) of ten No actors moon-viewing at the house of Nakayama Mosuke, a foot soldier, in Sayanomoto.

Beginning with Naotsuka Kanzaemon they all began to make fun of the foot soldier Araki Kyozaemen because he was so short. Araki became angry, killed Kanzaemon with his sword, and then began striking at the others.

Though he suffered a severed hand, Matsumoto Rokuzaemon came down into the garden, seized Araki from behind with his other hand, and said, "As for the likes of you, I'll twist your head off with one hand!" Grabbing away Araki's sword, he pushed him to the doorsill and pressed him down with his knee, but as he seized him by the neck he became faint and was quickly overpowered.

Araki quickly sprang back and again began to strike at those around him, but now Master Hayata (later known as Jirozaemon) met him with a spear. In the end he was overpowered by a number of men. Following this, Araki was made to commit seppuku, and the others who were involved were all made ronin on account of their indiscretion, but Hayata was later pardoned.

As Tsunetomo does not remember this story clearly, one should ask around about it.

Some years ago there was a sutra reading at the Jissoin in Kawakami. Five or six men from Kon'yamachi and the area of Tashiro had gone to the service, and on their way home passed some time drinking. Among them was one of Kizuka Kyuzaemon's retainers who, having some reason for doing so, turned down his companions' invitation to join them and returned borne before nightfall. The others, however, later pot into a fight with some men and cut them all down.

Kyuzaemon's retainer heard of this late that night and went quickly to his companions' quarters. He listened to the details and then said, "In the end I suppose you will have to submit a statement. When you do, you should say that I was there also and assisted in cutting down those men. When I return, I will say as much to Kyuzaemon. Since a fight is a matter involving all concerned, I should meet the same death sentence as you. And that is my deepest desire. The reason is that even if I were to explain to my master that I had returned home early, he would never accept it as the truth. Kyuzaemon has always been a severe man, and even if I were cleared by the investigators, he would probably have me executed as a coward right before his eyes. In such a case, dying with the bad reputation of having run away from a place would be extremely regretful.

"Since the fate of dying is the same, I would like to die being blamed for having killed a man. If you are not in agreement with this, I will cut my stomach open right here."

Having no alternative, his companions spoke as he had requested. Presently, during the inquiry, although the circumstances were explained in the above manner, it became known that the retainer had returned home early. All the investigators were impressed and in fact praised the man. This matter was transmitted to me only in outline, so I will look into the details at a later date.

Once when Nabeshima Aki no kami Shigetake was halfway through his meal, a guest suddenly came to see him and he left his tray just as it was. Later, a certain retainer of his sat down at the tray and began eating the fried fish that was on it. Just then Lord Aki came back and saw him, and the man became flustered and ran off. Lord Aki yelled out, "What a low-life slave you are to eat something that someone else has been eating!" and sat down and finished what was left.

This is one of Jin'emon's stories. It is said that this retainer was one of those who committed tsuifuku for the master.

Yamamoto Jin'emon always said to his retainers, "Go ahead and gamble and lie. A person who will not tell you seven lies within a hundred yards is useless as a man. " Long ago people spoke in this fashion because they were only concerned with a man's attitude towards military matters and considered that a man who was "correct" would never do great works. They also ignored the misconduct of men and dismissed such matters by saying, "They do good works, too... "

Men like Sagara Kyoma also excused retainers who had committed theft and adultery and trained them gradually. He said, "If it weren't for such persons, we would have no useful men at all."

Ikumo Oribe said, "If a retainer will just think about what he is to do for the day at hand, he will be able to do anything. If it is a single day's work, one should be able to put up with it. Tomorrow, too, is but a single day."

At the time when Lord Nabeshima Tsunashige had still not taken over as heir, he was converted by the Zen priest Kurotakiyama Choon and learned Buddhism from him. Since he had had an enlightenment, the priest was going to confer the seal upon him, and this became known throughout the mansion. At that time Yamamoto Gorozaemon had been ordered to be both Tsunashige's attendant and overseer. When he heard of this, he knew that it absolutely would not do and planned to make a request to Choon, and if he did not assent, kill him. He went to the priest's house in Edo and entered; the priest, thinking that he was someone on a pilgrimage, met him in a dignified manner.

Gorozaemon drew near him and said, ' 'I have some secret thing to tell you directly. Please send out your attendant priests.

"It is said that you will soon award Tsunashige the seal because of his cleverness in Buddhism. Now as you are from Hizen, you should know in large part the customs of the Ryuzoji and Nabeshima clans. Our country is ruled with harmony between high and low because, unlike others, it has had continuous heirs for successive generations. There has never been the taking of a Buddhist seal by the daimyo for ages past. If you present the seal now, Tsunashige will probably think of himself as enlightened and regard what his retainers say as so much dirt. A great man will become vain. Absolutely do not give this award. If you do not agree to this, I too am resolved. This he said with determination.

The priest's color changed, but he said, "Well, well. You have trustworthy intentions, and I see that you understand the affairs of your clan well. You are a loyal retainer..."

But Gorozaemon said, "No! I understand that ploy. I didn't come here to be praised. Without adding anything else, let me hear clearly whether you plan to cancel the seal or not."

Choon said, "What you say is reasonable. I will definitely not award the seal."

Gorozaemon made sure of this and returned. Tsunetomo heard this story directly from Gorozaemon.

A group of eight samurai all took the same road for some merrymaking. Two of them, Komori Eijun and Otsubo Jin'emon, went into a teahouse in front of the Kannon temple at Asakusa, got into an argument with the male employees there, and were soundly beaten. This could be heard by the others, who were in an excursion boat, and

Mute Rokuemen said, "We should go back and take revenge." Yoshii Yoichiemon and Ezoe Jinbei both agreed to this.

The others, however, dissuaded them, saying, "This will cause trouble for the clan," and they all returned home. When they arrived at the mansion, Rokuemon again said, "We should definitely take revenge!" but the others dissuaded him. Although they sustained heavy wounds on their arms and legs, Eijian and Jin'emon cut the teahouse men down, and those who had returned were taken to task by the master.

In due course some thought was given to the details of this event. One person said, "By waiting to get the agreement of others, a matter like taking revenge will never be brought to a conclusion. One should have the resolution to go alone and even to be cut down. A person who speaks vehemently about taking revenge but does nothing about it is a hypocrite. Clever people, by using their mouths alone, are taking care of their reputations for a later date. But a real stalwart is a man who will go out secretly, saying nothing, and die. It is not necessary to achieve one's aim; one is a stalwart in being cut down. Such a person will most likely achieve his purpose."

Ichiyuken was a low class servant in the kitchen of Lord Takanobu. Because of some grudge he had over a matter of wrestling, he cut down seven or eight men and was hence ordered to commit suicide. But when Lord Takanobu heard of this he pardoned the man and said, "In these strife torn times of our country, brave men are important. This man would seem to be a man of bravery." Consequently, at the time of the action around the Uji River, Lord Takanobu took Ichiyuken along, and the latter earned unrivaled fame, advancing deep into the lead and plundering the enemy every time.

At the battle of Takagi, Ichiyuken went so far into the enemy lines that Lord Takanobu felt regret and called him back. Since the vanguard had been unable to advance, only by quickly dashing out was he able to grab Ichiyuken by the sleeve of his armor. At that time Ichiyuken's head had suffered many wounds, but he had stopped them up with preen leaves which he bound with a thin towel.

On the first day of the attack on Hara Caste, Tsuruta Yashichibei went as a messenger from Lord Mimasaka to Oki Hyobu, but as he was delivering the message, he was shot through the pelvic region by a bullet fired from the castle and instantly fell on his face. He got up again and delivered the rest of the message, was felled a second time, and died. Yashichibei's body was carried back by Taira Chihyoei. When Chihyoei was returning to Hyobu's camp, he too was struck by a rifle ball and died.

Dense was born in Taku, and the members of his family living at this time were his elder brother Jirbei, his younger brother and his mother. Around the ninth month Denko's mother took Jirobei's son with her to hear a sermon. When it was time to go home, the child, as he was putting on his straw sandals, accidentally stepped on the foot of the man next to him. The man rebuked the child, and in the end they pot into a vehement argument and the man unsheathed his short sword and killed him. Jirobei's mother was dumb struck. She clung to the man, and he killed her too. Having done this, the man returned to his house.

This man's name was Gorouemon, and he was the son of a ronin by the name of Nakajima Moan. His younger brother was the mountain ascetic, Chuzobo. Moan was an advisor to Master Mimasaka, and Gorouemon had been given a stipend also.

When the circumstances became known at Jirobei's home, his younger brother set out for Gorouemon's place. Finding that the door was locked from within and that no one would come out, he disguised his voice, pretending to be a visitor. When the door was opened, he shouted his real name and crossed swords with his enemy. Both men fumbled into the rubbish heap, but in the end Gorouemon was killed. At this point, Chuzobo dashed in and cut down Jirobei's younger brother.

Hearing of this incident, Dense went immediately to Jirobei's place and said, "Of our enemies only one has been killed, while we have lost three. This is extremely regrettable, so why don't you strike at Chuzobo?" Jirobei, however, would not comply.

Denko felt that this was indeed shameful, and although a Buddhist priest, he decided on striking at the enemy of his mother, younger brother and nephew. He knew, nevertheless, that since he was simply an ordinary priest, there was likely to be a reprisal from Master Mimasaka and therefore worked hard, finally gaining eminence as the chief priest of the Ryuunji. He then went to the sword maker Iyonojo and asked him to make both a long and a short sword, offered to be his apprentice, and was even allowed to take part in the work.

By the twenty-third day of the ninth month of the following year, he was ready to make his departure. By chance a guest had come at this time. Giving orders for food to be served, Denko secretly slipped out of the chief priest's headquarters disguised as a layman. He then went to taku and, upon asking about Chuzobo, learned that he was with a large group of people who had gathered to watch the moonrise, and that therefore nothing much could be done. Unwilling to let time pile up, he felt that it would be fulfilling his basic desire to strike at the father, Moan. Going to Moan's house, he forced his way into the sleeping chambers, announced his name, and when the man began to get up, stabbed and killed him. When the people of the neighborhood came running and surrounded him, he explained the situation, threw away both long and short swords, and returned home. News of this preceded him to Saga, and a good number of Denko's parishioners came out quickly and accompanied him on his return.

Master Mimasaka was quite outraged, but as Denko was the chief priest of a Nabeshima clan temple, there was nothing to be done. Finally, through the offices of Nabeshima Toneri, he sent word to Tannen, the chief priest of the Kodenji, saying, "When a priest has killed a man, he should be given a sentence of death." Tannen's reply was, "The punishment for one within the religion will be in accordance with the feelings of the Kodenji. Kindly do not interfere."

Master Mimasaka became even angrier and asked, "What sort of punishment will this be?" Tannen replied, "Although it is profitless for you to know, you are forcing the question, so I will give you an answer. The [Buddhist] Law is that an apostate priest is deprived of his robes and driven out."

Denko's robes were taken from him at the Kodenji, and when he was to be driven out, some novices put on their long and short swords, and a great number of parishioners came to protect him, accompanying him as far as Todoroki. On the road a number of men who looked like hunters appeared and asked if the party had come from Taku. Thereafter Denko lived in Chikuzen, was well received by all, and was on friendly terms with samurai as well. This story was widely circulated, and it is said that he was treated kindly everywhere.

Horie San'emon's misdeed was robbing the Nabeshima warehouse in Edo of its money and fleeing to another province. He was caught and confessed. Thus it was pronounced, "Because this is a grave crime he should be tortured to death, " and Nakano Daigaku was ordered to be the official who verified the execution. At first all the hairs on his body were burner off and his fingernails were pulled out. His tendons were then cut, he was bored with drills and subjected to various other tortures. Throughout, he did not flinch once, nor did his face change color. In the end his back was split, he was boiled in soy sauce, and his body was bent back in two.

Once when Fukuchi Rokurouemon was leaving the castle, the palanquin of what appeared to be a rather upper class woman was passing in front of Master Taku's mansion, and a man who was standing there made the proper salutation. A halberd carrier who was with the palanquin procession, however, said to the man, "You didn't bow low enough," and struck him on the head with the handle of his halberd. When the man wiped his head, he found that he was bleeding. In just that condition he stood up and said, "You have committed an outrageous act, even though I was courteous. A regrettable piece of luck." So saying, he cut the halberd carrier down with a single blow. The palanquin continued on to wherever it was going, but Rokurouemon unsheathed his spear, stood before the man, and said. "Put away your sword. Within the castle grounds it is forbidden to go about holding a naked blade." The man said, "What happened now was unavoidable, and I was compelled by the circumstances. Certainly you could see that this was so. Although I would like to sheathe my sword, it is difficult to do so due to the tone of your words. It is unpleasant, but I shall be glad to accept your challenge."

Rokurouemon immediately threw down his spear and said courteously, "What you have said is reasonable. My name is Fukuchi Rokurouemon. I will bear witness that your conduct was quite admirable. Moreover, I will back you up even if it means forfeiting my life. Now put away your sword."

"With pleasure," the man said, and sheathed his sword. On being asked where he was from, the man replied that he was a retainer of Taku Nagato no kami Yasuyori. Therefore Rokurouemon accompanied him and explained the circumstances. Knowing that the woman in the palanquin was the wife of a nobleman, however, Lord Nagato ordered his retainer to commit seppuku.

Rokurouemon came forward and said, "Because I have given the promise of a samurai, if this man is ordered to commit seppuku, then I will commit seppuku first."

It is said that the affair was thus finished without mishap.

Lord Shima sent a messenger to his father, Lord Aki, saying, "I would like to make a pilgrimage to the Atago Shrine in Kyoto." Lord Aki asked, "For what reason?" and the messenger replied, "Since Atago is the pod of archery, my intentions are for the sake of fortune in war." Lord Aki became angry and answered. "That is absolutely worthless! Should the vanguard of the Nabeshimas be making requests to Atago? If the incarnation of Atago were fighting on the enemy's side, the vanguard should be equal to cutting him neatly in two."

Dohaku lived in Kurotsuchibaru. His son was named Gorobei. Once when Gorobei was carrying a load of rice, a ronin of Master

Kumashiro Sakyo's by the name of Iwamura Kyunai was coming from the other direction. There was a grudge between the two of them from some former incident, and now Gorobei struck Kyunai with his load of rice, started an argument, beat him and pushed him into a ditch, and then returned home. Kyunai yelled some threat at Gorobei and returned to his home where he related this event to his older brother Gen'emon. The two of them then went off' to Gorobei's to take revenge.

When they got there the door was open just a bit, and Gorobei was waiting behind it with drawn sword. Not knowing this, Gen'emon entered and Gorobei struck at him with a sweep from the side. having received a deep wound, Gen'emon used his sword as a staff and hobbled back outside. Then Kyunai rushed in and struck at Dohaku's son-in-law Katsuemon, who was sitting by the hearth. His sword glanced off the pot hanger, and he cut off half of Katsuemen's face. Dohaku, together with his wife, grabbed the sword away from Kyunai.

Kyunai apologized and said, "I have already achieved my purpose. Please give me back my sword and I will accompany my brother home. But when Dohaku banded it back to him, Kyunai cut him once in the back and severed his neck halfway through. He then crossed swords with Gorobei again and both went outside and fought an even match until he cut off Gorobei's arm.

At this point Kyunai, who also suffered many wounds, shouldered his elder brother Gen'emon and returned home. Gen'emon, however, died on the way back.

Gorobei's wounds were numerous. Although he stopped the bleeding, he died on account of drinking some water. Dohaku's wife suffered some severed fingers. Dohaku's wound was a severed neck bone, and since only his throat remained intact, his head hung down in front. Now boosting his head up with his own hands, Dohaku went off to the surgeons.

The surgeons treatment was like this: First he rubbed a mixture of pine resin and oil on Dohaku's jaw and bound it in ramie. He then attached a rope to the top of his head and tied it to a beam, sewed the open wound shut, and buried his body in rice so that he would not be able to move.

Dohaku never lost consciousness nor did he change from his everyday attitude, nor did he even drink ginseng. It is said that only on the third day when there was a hemorrhage did he use a little medicinal stimulant. In the end the bones mended, and he recovered without incident.

When Lord Mitsushige contracted smallpox at Shimonoseki, Ikushima Sakuan gave him some medicine. It was an exceptionally heavy case of smallpox, and his attendants both high and low were rather tense. Suddenly his scabs turned black. The men who were nursing him lost heart and secretly informed Sakuan, who came immediately. He said, "Well, this is something to be thankful for. The scabs are healing. He should soon make a complete recovery with no complications. I give you my guarantee."

The people who were at Lord Mitsushige's side heard this and thought, "Sakuan looks a little deranged. This has become all the more hopeless."

Sakuan then set folding screens around, came out after a while, and fed Lord Mitsushige one packet of medicine. Very quickly the patient's scabs healed, and he made a complete recovery. Sakuan later confided to someone, "I gave the master that one packet of medicine resolved that, as I was undertaking this treatment alone, if he did not recover I would quickly cut open my stomach and die with him."

When Nakano Takumi was dying, his whole house gathered and he said, "You should understand that there are three conditions to the resolution of a retainer. They are the condition of the master's will, the condition of vitality, and the condition of one's death."

Once when a number of men had gathered on the platform of the inner citadel of the castle, a certain man said to Uchida Shouemon, "It is said that you are a teacher of the sword, but judging by your everyday attitude, your teaching must be very wild indeed. If you were requested to perform kaishaku, I can imagine that instead of cutting the neck you'd probably cut the top of the man's head."

Shouemon rejoined, "Such is not the case. Draw a little ink spot on your own neck, and I'll show you that I can cut without being off by a hair."

Nagayama Rokurozaemon was going down the Tokaido and was at Hamamatsu. As he passed by an inn, a beggar faced his palanquin and said, "I am a ronin from Echigo. I am short of money and in difficulties. We are both warriors. Please help me

out."

Rokurozaemon got angry and said, "It is a discourtesy to mention that we are both warriors. If I were in your state of affairs, I'd cut my stomach open. Rather than being out of money for the road and exposing yourself to shame, cut your stomach open right where you are!" It is said that the beggar moved off.

In Makiguchi Yohei's life he was kaishaku for many men. When a certain Kanahara was to commit seppuku, Yohei consented to be kaishaku. Kanahara thrust the sword into his belly, but at the point of pulling it across he was unable to go further. Yohei approached his side, yelled "Ei!" and stamped his foot. From this impetus, Kanahara was able to pull his sword straight across his belly. After finishing the kaishaku, it is said that Yohei shed tears and said, "Even though he was formerly a good friend of mine..." This is a story of Master Sukeemon's.

At the time of a certain person's seppuku, when the kaishaku a cut off his head, a little bit of skin was left hanging and the head was not entirely separated from the body. The official observer said, "There's some left." The kaishaku got angry, took hold of the head, and cutting it completely off, held it above eye level and said, "Take a look!" It is said that it was rather chilling. This is a story of Master Sukeemon's.

In the practice of past times, there were instances when the head flew off'. It was said that it is best to cut leaving a little skin remaining so that it doesn't fly oft in the direction of the verifying officials. However, at present it is best to cut clean through.

A man who had cut off fifty heads once said, "According to the head, there are cases when even the trunk of a body will bring some reaction to you. Cutting off just three heads, at first there is no reaction and you can cut well. But when you get to four or five, you feel quite a bit of reaction. At any rate, since this is a very important matter, if one always plans on bringing the head to the ground there should be no mistakes."

When Lord Nabeshima Tsunashige was a child, Iwamura Kuranosuke was ordered to the position of elder. On one occasion Kuranosuke saw that there were gold coins before the young Tsunashige and asked the attending retainer, "For what reason have you brought these out before the young master?" The attendant replied, "The master just now heard that a gift had been brought for him. He said that he had not yet seen it, so I brought it out for him." Kuranosuke scolded the man severely, saying, "To place such base things before a person of importance is the extremity of careless ness. You may also consider them something not to be put before the lord's son. Attending retainers should henceforth be very mindful of this."

Another time, when Lord Tsunashige was about twenty years old, he once went to the mansion at Naekiyama for some diversion. As the party neared the mansion, he asked for a walking stick. His sandal carrier, Miura Jibuzaemon, fashioned a stick and was about to give it to the young lord.

Kuranosake saw this, quickly took the stick from Jibuzaemon, and scolded him severely, saying, ' 'Will you make our important young lord a sluggard? Even if he should ask for a stick, it should not be given to him. This is carelessness on the part of the attending retainer."

Jibuzaernon was later promoted to the rank of teakiyari, and Tsunetomo heard this story directly from him.

CHAPTER 9

When Shimomura Shoun

WHEN Shimomura Shoun was on service at the castle, Lord Naoshige said, "How wonderful it is that Katsushige is so vigorous and powerful for his age. In wrestling with his peers he even beat those who are older than he is."

Shoun replied, "Even though I'm an old man, I'll bet I'm best at seated wrestling." So saying, he jerked up Katsushige and threw him so forcefully that it hurt. He then said, "To be prideful about your strength while your mettle is not yet established is likely to bring you shame in the midst of people. You are weaker than you look." Then he withdrew.

At the time when Matsuda Yohei was an intimate friend of Ishii Jinku's, there developed some bad feelings between the former and Nozoe Jinbei. Yohei sent word to Jinbei saying, "Please come and I will settle this matter once and for all." Then he and Jinku set out together and, coming to the Yamabushi mansion at Kihara, they crossed the only bridge there was and destroyed it. Talking over the circumstances of the discord, they examined them from all sides and found no reason to fight. But when they decided to turn around and go home, there was, of course, no bridge.

While they were looking for an appropriate way of crossing the moat, the men whom the two had challenged could be seen approaching stealthily. Yohei and Jinku saw this and said, "We have passed the point of no return, and may as well fight rather than be disgraced at a later date." The battle lasted for some time. Seriously wounded, Yohei fell down between two fields. Jinbei also received a deep wound, and with blood flowing into his eyes was unable to find Yohei. While Jinbei thus searched about blindly, Yohei was able to hold him off from his prone position and in the end cut him down. But when he attempted to deliver the finishing blow, having no strength left in his hand, he pierced Jinbei's neck by pushing the sword with his foot.

At this point, friends arrived and accompanied Yohei back. After his wounds healed he was ordered to commit seppuku. At that time he called his friend Jinku, and they drank a farewell cup together.

Okubo Toemon of Shioda ran a wine shop for Nabeshima Kenmotsu. Lord Okura, the son of Nabeshima Kai no kami, was a cripple and confined indoors in a place called Mine. He harbored wrestlers and liked rowdies. The wrestlers would often go to nearby villages and cause disturbances. One time they went to Toemon's place, drank sake and talked unreasonably, bringing Toemon into an argument. He met them with a halberd, but as there were two of them he was cut down.

His son, Kannosuke, was fifteen years old and was in the midst of studies at the Jozeiji when he was informed of the incident. Galloping off, he took a short sword about sixteen inches in length, joined combat with the two big men, and in a short time finished them both off. Although Kannosuke received thirteen wounds, he recovered. Later he was called Doko and is said to have become very adept at massage.

It is said that Tokunaga Kichizaemon repeatedly complained, "I've grown so old that now, even if there were to be a battle, I wouldn't be able to do anything. Still, I would like to die by galloping into the midst of the enemy and being struck down and killed. It would be a shame to do nothing more than to die in one's bed." It is said that the priest Gyojaku heard this when he was an acolyte. Gyojaku's master was the priest Yemen, who was Kichizaemon's youngest child.

When Sagara Kyuma was requested to become a chief retainer, he said to Nabeshima Heizaemon, "For some reason I have been increasingly well treated by the master and now have been requested to take a high rank. Not having a good retainer, my affairs are liable to be in disorder. It is my request that you give me your retainer, Takase Jibusaemon." Heizaemon listened to him and consented, saying, "It is very gratifying that you have kept an eye on my retainer. I will therefore do as you ask."

But when he related this to Jibusaemon, the latter said, "I should reply directly to Master Kyuma." He then went to Kyuma's place and talked with him. Jibusaemon told Kyuma, "I know it is a great honor that you have thought well of me and have made this request. But a retainer is a person who cannot change masters. As you are of high rank, if I were to become your retainer my life would be replete, but that repleteness would be a vexation to me. Because Her zaemon is of low rank and is hard pressed, we live by eating cheap rice gruel. Yet that is sweet enough. Please think this over." Kyuma was extremely impressed.

A certain man went of somewhere and on returning home late at night, found that a strange man had slipped into the house and was committing adultery with his wife. He thereupon killed the man. He then broke down a wall and propped up a bale of rice, and by this arrangement submitted to the authorities that he had killed a thief. Thus it went without mishap. After some time had passed he divorced his wife and the affair was finished.

When a certain person returned home from some place or other, he found his wife committing adultery with a retainer in the bedroom. When he drew near the two, his retainer fled through the kitchen. He then went into the bedroom and slew his wife.

Calling the maidservant, he explained what had happened and said, "Because this would bring shame to the children, it should be covered up as death by illness and I will need considerable help. If you think that this is too much for you, I may as well kill you too for your part in this serious crime."

She replied, "If you will spare my life, I will go on as if I don't know anything. " She rearranged the room and set out the corpse in its nightclothes. Then, after sending a man to the doctor's place two or three times saying that there was a sudden illness, they sent a last messenger saying that it was too late and there was no longer any need to come. The wife's uncle was called in and told about the illness, and he was convinced. The entire affair was passed off as death by illness, and to the end no one knew the truth. At a later date the retainer was dismissed. This affair happened in Edo.

At New Year's in the third year of Keicho at a place in Korea called Yolsan, when the armies of the Ming appeared by the hundreds of thousands, the Japanese troops were amazed and watched with bated breath. Lord Naoshige said, "Well, well. That's a great number of men ! I wonder how many hundreds of thousands there are?"

Jin'emon said, "In Japan, for something that's numberless we say 'as many as the hairs on a three-year old calf.' This would certainly live up to the number of hairs on a three-year-old calf!" It is said that everybody laughed and regained their spirits.

Later, Lord Katsushige was hunting at Ml. Shiroishi and told Nakano Matabei about this. ' 'Except for your father who spoke in such a way, there was no one who said even a word."

Nakano Jin'emon constantly said, "A person who serves when treated kindly by the master is not a retainer. But one who serves when the master is being heartless and unreasonable is a retainer. You should understand this principle well."

When Yamamoto Jin'emon was eighty years old, he became ill. At one point, he seemed to be on the verge of groaning, and someone said to him, "You'll feel better if you groan. Go ahead. *' But he replied, "Such is not the case. The name of Yamamoto Jin'emon is known by everyone, and I have shown up well throughout a whole lifetime. To let people hear my groaning voice in my last moments would never do." It is said that he did not let out a groan to the very end.

A certain son of Mori Monbei got into a fight and returned home wounded. Asked by Monbei, "What did you do to your opponent?" his son replied, "I cut him down."

When Monbei asked, "Did you deliver the coup de grace?" his son replied, "Indeed I did."'

Then Monbei said, "You have certainly done well, and there is nothing to regret. Now, even if you fled you would have to commit seppuku anyway. When your mood improves, commit seppuku, and rather than die by another's hand, you can die by your father's." And soon after he performed kaishaku for his son.

A man in the same group as Aiura Genzaemon committed some nefarious deed, and so the group leader gave him a note, condemning him to death, which was to be taken to Genzaemon's place. Genzaemon perused the note and then said to the man, "It says here that I should kill you, so I will do away with you on the eastern bank. Previously you have practiced such things as swordsmanship.. . . Now fight with all you've got."

The man replied, "I will do as you say," and with Genzaemon alone accompanying him, they left the house. They had gone about twenty yards along the edge of the moat when a retainer of Genzaernon's yelled out, "Hey, Hey!" from the other side. As Genzaemon was turning around, the condemned man attacked him with his sword. Genzaemon ducked backwards, drew his sword, and cut the man down. He then returned home.

He put the clothes he had been wearing at that time into a chest and locked them up, never showing them to anyone for the rest of his life. After he died the clothes were examined, and it was seen that they were rent. This was told by his son, Genzaemon.

Okubo Doko is said to have remarked:

Everyone says that no masters of the arts will appear as the world comes to an end. This is something that I cannot claim to understand. Plants such as peonies, azaleas and camellias will be able to produce beautiful flowers, end of the world or not. If men would give some thought to this fact, they would understand. And if people took notice of the masters of even these times, they would be able to say that there are masters in the various arts. But people become imbued with the idea that the world has come to an end and no longer put forth any effort. This is a shame. There is no fault in the times.

While Fukahori Magoroku was still living as a dependent second son, he once went hunting at Fukahori, and his retainer, mistaking him for a wild boar in the darkness of the undergrowth, fired the rifle, wounding him in the knee and causing him to fall from a great height. The retainer, greatly upset, stripped himself to the waist and was about to commit seppuku. Magoroku said, "You can cut your stomach open later. I don't feel well, so bring me some water to drink." The retainer ran about and obtained some water for his master to drink and in the process calmed down. After that the retainer was again about to commit seppuku, but Magoroku forcibly stopped him. Upon returning they checked in with the man on guard, and Magoroku asked his father, Kanzaemen, to forgive the retainer.

Kanzaemon said to the retainer, "It was an unexpected mistake, so do not be worried. There is no need for reservation. Continue with your work."

A man by the name of Takagi got into an argument with three farmers in the neighborhood, was soundly beaten out in the fields, and returned home. His wife said to him, "Haven't you forgotten about the matter of death?" "Definitely not!" he replied.

His wife then retorted, "At any rate, a man dies only once. Of the various ways of dying - dying of disease, being cut down in battle, seppuku or being beheaded - to die ignominiously would be a shame," and went outside. She soon returned, carefully put the two children to bed, prepared some torches, dressed herself for battle after nightfall, and then said, "When I went out to survey the scene a bit earlier, it seemed that the three men went into one place for a discussion. Now is the right time. Let's go quickly!" So saying, they went out with the husband in the lead, burning torches and wearing short swords. They broke into their opponents' place and dispersed them, both husband and wife slashing about and killing two of the men and wounding the other. The husband was later ordered to commit seppuku.

CHAPTER 10

There was a certain retainer

THERE WAS a certain retainer of Ikeda Shingen's who started an argument with a man, grappled him to the ground, thrashed him soundly, and trampled on him until his companions ran up and pulled them apart. The elders conferred over this and said, "The man who was trampled should be punished." Shingen heard this and said, "A fight is something that goes to the finish. A man who forgets the Way of the Samurai and does not use his sword will be forsaken by the gods and Buddhas. As an example to subsequent retainers, both men should be crucified." The men who had pulled them apart were banished.

In Yui Shosetsu's military instructions, "The Way of the Three Ultimates," there is a passage on the character of karma.' He received an oral teaching of about eighteen chapters concerning the Greater Bravery and the Lesser Bravery. He neither wrote them down nor committed them to memory but rather forgot them completely. Then, in facing real situations, he acted on impulse and the things that he had learned became wisdom of his own. This is the character of karma.

When faced with a crisis, if one puts some spittle on his earlobe and exhales deeply through his nose, he will overcome anything at hand. This is a secret matter. Furthermore, when experiencing a rush of blood to the head, if one puts spittle on the upper part of one's ear, it will soon go away.

Tzu Ch'an was on the point of death when someone asked him how to govern the country. He replied:

There is nothing that surpasses ruling with benevolence. However, to put into practice enough benevolent governing to rule the country is difficult. To do this lukewarmly will result in neglect. If governing with benevolence is difficult, then it is best to govern strictly. To govern strictly means to be strict before things have arisen, and to do things in such a way that evil will not arise. To be strict after the evil has arisen is like laying a snare. There are few people who will make mistakes with fire after having once been burned. Of people who regard water lightly, many have been drowned.

A certain man said, "I know the shapes of Reason and of Woman." When asked about this, he replied, "Reason is four cornered and will not move even in an extreme situation. Woman is round. One can say that she does not distinguish between good and evil or right and wrong and tumbles into any place at all."

The basic meaning of etiquette is to be quick at both the beginning and end and tranquil in the middle. Mitani Chizaemon heard this and said, "That's just like being a kaishaku.

Fukae Angen accompanied an acquaintance of his to the priest Tesshu of Osaka, and at first said privately to the priest, "This man aspires to study Buddhism and hopes to receive your teaching. He is a man of rather high determination."

Soon after the interview the priest said, "Angen is a man who does harm to others. He said that this man is a good man, but wherein is his goodness? There was no goodness visible to Tesshu's eyes. It is not a good idea to praise people carelessly.

When praised, both wise and foolish become prideful. To praise is to do harm."

When Hotta Kaga no kami Masamori was a page to the shogun, he was so headstrong that the shogun wished to test what was at the bottom of his heart. To do this, the shogun heated a pair of tongs and placed them in the hearth. Masamori's custom was to go to the other side of the hearth, take the tongs, and greet the master. This time, when he unsuspectingly picked up the tongs, his hands were immediately turned. As he did obeisance in his usual manner, however, the shogun quickly pot up and took the tongs from him.

A certain person said, "When a castle is being surrendered, as long as there are one or two men within it who are determined to hold on, the defending forces will not be of one accord, and in the end no one will hold the castle. "In the taking of the castle, if when the man who is to receive it approaches and the one or two men who are determined to hold on to it lightly fire on him from the shadows, the man will be alarmed and the battle will be on. In such a case, even though it is unwillingly done, the castle will have to be stormed. This is called being forced to besiege a castle by those besieged."

The Buddhist priest Ryozan wrote down some generalities concerning Takanobu's battles. A certain priest saw this and criticized him, saying, "It is inappropriate for a priest to write about a military commander. No matter how successful his writing style may be, since he is not acquainted with military things, he is liable to be mistaken in understanding a famous general's mind. It is irreverent to pass on misconceptions concerning a famous general to later generations."

A certain person said, "In the Saint's mausoleum there is a poem that goes:

"If in one's heart He follows the path of sincerity, Though he does not pray Will not the gods protect him? What is this path of sincerity?"

A man answered him by saying, "You seem to like poetry. I will answer you with a poem.

As everything in this world is but a shame, Death is the only sincerity. It is said that becoming as a dead man in one's daily living is the following of the path of sincerity."

If you cut a face lengthwise, urinate on it, and trample on it with straw sandals, it is said that the skin will come off. This was heard by the priest Gyojaku when he was in Kyoto. It is information to be treasured.

One of Matsudaira Sagami no kami's retainers went to Kyoto on a matter of debt collection and took up lodgings by renting living quarters in a townhouse. One day while standing out front watching the people go by, he heard a passerby say, "They say that Lord Matsudaira's men are involved in a fight right now." The retainer thought, "How worrisome that some of my companions are involved in a fight. There are some men to relieve those at Edo staying here. Perhaps these are the men involved." He asked the passerby of the location, but when he arrived out of breath, his companions had already been cut down and their adversaries were at the point of delivering the coup de grace. He quickly let out a yell, cut the two men down, and returned to his lodgings.

This matter was made known to an official of the shogunate, and the man was called up before him and questioned. "You gave assistance in your companions' fight and thus disregarded the government's ordinance. This is true beyond a doubt, isn't it?"

The man replied, "I am from the country, and it is difficult for me to understand everything that Your Honor is saying. Would you please repeat that?"

The official got angry and said, "Is there something wrong with your ears? Didn't you abet a fight, commit bloodshed, disregard the government's ordinance, and break the law?"

The man then replied, "I have at length understood what you are saying. Although you say that I have broken the law and disregarded the government's ordinance, I have by no means done so. The reason for this is that all living things value their lives, and this goes without saying for human beings. I, especially, value my life. However, I thought that to hear a rumor that one's friends are involved in a fight and to pretend not to hear this is not to preserve the Way of the Samurai, so I ran to the place of action. To shamelessly return home after seeing my friends struck down would surely have lengthened my life, but this too would be disregarding the Way. In observing the Way, one will throw away his own precious life. Thus, in order to preserve the Way of the Samurai and not to disregard the Samurai Ordinances, I quickly threw away my life at that place. I beg that you execute me immediately."

The official was very impressed and later dismissed the matter, communicating to Lord Matsudaira, "You have a very able samurai in your service. Please treasure him."

This is among the sayings of the priest Banker. "Not to borrow the strength of another, nor to rely on one's own strength; to cut off past and future thoughts, and not to live within the everyday mind... then the Great Way is right before one's eyes."

Lord Soma's family genealogy, called the Chiken marokashi, was the best in Japan. One year when his mansion suddenly caught fire and was burning to the ground, Lord Soma said, "I feel no regret about the house and all its furnishings, even if they burn to the very last piece, because they are things that can be replaced later on. I only regret that I was unable to take out the genealogy, which is my family's most precious treasure." There was one samurai among those attending him who said, "I will go in and take it out."

Lord Soma and the others all laughed and said, "The house is already engulfed in flames. How are you going to take it out?"

Now this man had never been loquacious, nor had he been particularly useful, but being a man who did things from beginning to end, he was engaged as an attendant. At this point he said, "I have never been of use to my master because I'm so careless, but I have lived resolved that someday my life should be of use to him. This seems to be that time." And he leapt into the flames. After the fire had been extinguished the master said, "Look for his remains. What a pity!"

Looking everywhere, they found his burnt corpse in the garden adjacent to the living quarters. When they turned it over, blood flowed out of the stomach. The man had cut open his stomach and placed the genealogy inside and it was not damaged at all. From this time on it was called the "Blood Genealogy.'

According to a certain person's story, "In the tradition of the I Ching, it is a mistake to think that it is something for divination. Its essence is non-divination. This can be seen by the fact that the Chinese character 'I' is read as 'change.' Although one divines good fortune, if he does evil it will become bad fortune. And although he divines bad fortune, if he does good it will become good fortune.

"Confucius' saying, 'By setting myself to the task for many years and in the end learning change [I], I should make no big mistakes,' is not a matter of learning the I Ching. It means by studying the essence of change and conducting oneself for many years in the Way of Good, one should make no mistakes."

Hirano Gonbei was one of the Men of Seven Spears who advanced straight up the hill at the battle of Shizugadake. At a later date he was invited to become one of Lord Ieyasu's hatamoto. Once he was being entertained at Master Hosekawa's. The master said, "Master Gonbei's bravery is not a hidden matter in Japan. It is truly a shame that such a man of bravery has been placed in a low rank such as you are in now. This must be contrary to your wishes. If you were to become a retainer of mine, I would give you half the domain."

Giving no answer at all, Gonbei suddenly pot up from his seat, went out to the veranda, stood facing the house, and urinated. Then he said, "If I were the master's retainer, it would never do to urinate from here."

When the priest Daiyu from Sanshu was making a sick call at a certain place, he was told, "The man has just now died." Daiyu said, "Such a thing shouldn't have happened at this time. Didn't this occur from insufficient treatment? What a shame!"

Now the doctor happened to be there at that time and heard what was said from the other side of the shoji. He got extraordinarily angry and came out and said, "I heard Your Reverence say that the man died from insufficient treatment. Since I am a rather bungling doctor, this is probably true. I have heard that a priest embodies the power of the Buddhist Law. Let me see you bring this dead man back to life, for without such evidence Buddhism is worthless."

Daiyu was put out by this, but he felt that it would be unpardonable for a priest to put a blemish on Buddhism, so he said, "I will indeed show you how to bring his life back by prayer. Fleas' wait a moment. I must go prepare myself," and returned to the temple. Soon he came back and sat in meditation next to the corpse. Pretty soon the dead man began to breathe and then completely revived. It is said that he lived on for another half a year. As this was something told directly to the priest Tannen, there is nothing mistaken about it.

When telling of the way he prayed, Daiyu said, "This is something not practiced in our sect, so I didn't know of any way of prayer. I simply set my heart for the sake of the Buddhist Law, returned to the temple, sharpened a short sword that had been given as an offering to the temple, and put it in my robe. Then I faced the dead man and prayed, 'If the strength of the Buddhist Law exists, come back to life immediately. 'Since I was thus committed, if he hadn't come back to life, I was resolved to the point of cutting open my stomach and dying embracing the corpse."

When Yamamoto Gorozaemon went to the priest Tetsugyu in Edo wanting to hear something about Buddhism, Tetsugyo said, "Buddhism gets rid of the discriminating mind. It is nothing more than this. I can give you an illustration in terms of the warrior. The Chinese character for "cowardice" is made by adding the character for "meaning" to the character radical for "mind". Now "meaning" is "discrimination," and when a man attaches discrimination to his true mind, he becomes a coward. In the Way of the Samurai can a man be courageous when discrimination arises? I suppose you can get the idea from this."

According to what one of the elders said, taking an enemy on the battlefield is like a hawk taking a bird. Even though it enters into the midst of a thousand of them, it gives no attention to any bird other than the one that it has first marked.

Moreover, what is called a tezuke no kubi is a head that one has taken after having made the declaration, "I will take that warrior wearing such and such armor."

In the Kiyogunkan one person said, "When facing the enemy, I feel as if I have just entered darkness. Because of this I get heavily wounded. Although you have fought with many famous men, you have never been wounded. Why is that?"

The other man answered, "When I have faced the enemy, of course it is like being in the dark. But if at that time I tranquilize my mind, it becomes like a night lit by a pale moon. If I begin my attack from that point, I feel as though I will not be wounded. "This is the situation at the moment of truth.

A rifle ball hitting the water will ricochet. It is said that if one marks it with a knife or dents it with his teeth, it will pass through the water. Moreover, when the master is hunting or some such thing, if one marks the ball with a sign, it will come in handy in case of a mishap.

When Master Owari, Master Kit and Master Mite were around the age of ten, one day Lord Ieyasu was with them in the garden and knocked down a big wasps' nest. A great number of wasps flew out, and Master Owari and Master Kit were frightened and ran away. But

Master Mite picked off the wasps that were on his face, threw them away one by one, and did not run away.

Another time, when Lord Ieyasu was roasting a great number of chestnuts in a large hearth, he invited the boys to join him. When the chestnuts got sufficiently hot, they all started to pop out at once. Two of the boys were frightened and moved away. Master Mite, however, not the least bit frightened, picked up the ones that had popped out and threw them back into the hearth.

In order to study medicine Eguchi Than went to old Yoshida Ichian's place in the Bancho area of Edo. At that time, there was in the neighborhood a teacher of swordsmanship, to whom he used to go for training from time to time. There was a ronin pupil there who one day came up to toan and said as a parting remark, "I am now going to realize a long cherished ambition, one I have had for many years. I am informing you of this because you have always been friendly to me." Then he walked away. Than felt uneasy about this, and when he followed him, he could see a man wearing a braided hat coming from the opposite direction.

Now the sword teacher was about eight or ten yards ahead of the ronin, and in passing by the man with the hat he soundly struck the man's scabbard with his own. When the man looked around, the ronin knocked off' the man's hat and announced in a loud voice that his purpose was revenge. With the man's attention being distracted by the confusion, he was easily cut down. A tremendous amount of congratulations came from the nearby mansions and townhouses. It is said that they even brought out money for him. This was a favorite story of Toan's.

Once when the priest Ungo of Matsushima was passing through the mountains at night, he was set upon by mountain bandits. Ungo said, "I am a man of this area, not a pilgrim. I have no money at all, but you can have these clothes if you like. Please spare my life."

The bandits said, "Well, our efforts have been in vain. We don't need anything like clothes," and passed on. They had gone about two hundred yards when Ungo turned back and called to them, "I have broken the commandment against lying. In my confusion I forgot that I had one piece of silver in my moneybag. I am truly regretful I said that I had nothing at all. I have it here now, so please take it." The mountain bandits were deeply impressed, cut off their hair right there, and became his disciples.

In Edo four or five hatamoto gathered together one night for a game of go. At one point one of them got up to go to the toilet, and while he was gone an argument broke out. One man was cut down, the lights were extinguished, and the place was in an uproar. When the man came running back, he yelled,

"Everybody calm down I This is really over nothing at all. Put the lamps back on and let me handle this." After the lamps had been relighted and everyone had calmed down, the man suddenly struck off the head of the other man involved in the argument. He then said, "My luck as a samurai having run out, I was not present at the fight. If this were seen as cowardice, I would be ordered to commit seppuku. Even if that didn't happen, I would have no excuse if it were said that I had fled to the toilet, and I would still have no recourse other than seppuku. I have done this thing because I thought I would die having cut down an adversary rather than die having shamed myself alone." When the shogun heard of this matter, he praised the man.

Once a group of ten blind masseuses were traveling together in the mountains, and when they began to pass along the top of a precipice, they all became very cautious, their legs shook, and they were in general struck with terror. Just then the leading man stumbled and fell of the cliff. Those that were left all wailed, "Ahh, ahh I How piteous!" But the masseuse who had fallen veiled up from below, "Don't be afraid. Although I fell, it was nothing. I am now rather at ease. Before falling I kept thinking 'What will I do if I fall?' and there was no end to my anxiety. But now I've settled down. If the rest of you want to be at ease, fall quickly!"

Hojo Awa no kami once gathered together his disciples in the martial arts and called in a physiognomist, who was popular in Edo at the time, to have him determine whether they were brave men or cowards. He had them see the man one by one, telling them, "If he determines 'bravery,' you should strive all the more. If it is 'cowardice,' you should strive by throwing away your life. It's something that you're born with, so there's no shame in it."

Hirose Denzaemon was then about twelve or thirteen years old. When he sat down in front of the physiognomist, he said in a bristling voice, "if you read cowardice in me, I'll cut you down with a single blow !"

When there is something to be said, it is better if it is said right away. If it is said later, it will sound like an excuse. Moreover, it is occasionally good to really overwhelm your opponent. Also, in addition to having spoken sufficiently it is the highest sort of victory to teach your opponent something that will be to his benefit. This is in accordance with the Way.

The priest Ryoi said: The samurai of old were mortified by the idea of dying in bed; they hoped only to die on the battlefield. A priest, too, will be unable to fulfill the Way unless he is of this disposition. The man who shuts himself away and avoids the company of men is a coward. Only evil thoughts allow one to imagine that something good can be done by shutting oneself away. For even if one does some good thing by shutting himself away, he will be unable to keep the way open for future generations by promulgating the clan traditions.

Takeda Shingen's retainer, Amari Bizen no kami, was killed in action and his son, Tozo, at the age of eighteen took over his father's position as an armed horseman attached to a general. Once a certain man in his group received a deep wound, and since the blood would not clot, Tozo ordered him to drink the feces of a red-haired horse mixed with water. The wounded man said, "Life is dear to me. How can I drink horse feces?' Tozo heard this and said, "What an admirably brave warrior ! What you say is reasonable. However, the basic meaning of loyalty requires us to preserve our lives and gain victory for our master on the battlefield. Well, then, I'll drink some for you." Then he drank some himself and banded over the cup to the man who took the medicine gratefully and recovered.

CHAPTER 11

In the "Notes on Martial Laws"

IN THE "Notes on Martial Laws" it is written that: The phrase, "Win first, fight later, " can be summed up in the two words, "Win beforehand." The resourcefulness of times of peace is the military preparation for times of war. With five hundred allies one can defeat an enemy force of ten thousand.

When advancing on the enemy's castle and then pulling back, do not retreat by the main road, but rather by the side roads.

One should lay ones dead and wounded allies face down in the direction of the enemy.

It is a matter of course that a warrior's attitude should be to be in the vanguard during an attack and in the rear during a retreat. In approaching for the attack he does not forget to wait for the right moment. In waiting for the right moment he never forgets the attack.

A helmet is usually thought to be very heavy, but when one is attacking a castle or something similar, and arrows, bullets, large rocks, great pieces of wood and the like are corning down, it will not seem the least bit so.

Once when Master Yagyu was before the shogun on some business, a number of bamboo swords fell from the ceiling. He quickly clasped his hands above his head and was not struck.

Again, at a certain time when he was summoned, the shogun was waiting behind cover with a bamboo sword ready to strike him. Master Yagyu called out in a loud voice, "This is for your own discipline. Don't look!" As the shogun turned around, Master Yagyu stepped up and took the sword out of his hand.

A person who does not want to be struck by the enemies arrows will have no divine protection. For a man who does not wish to be hit by the arrows of a common soldier, but rather by those of a warrior of fame, there will be the protection for which he has asked.

Wind-bells are things that are used during campaigns in order to know the direction of the wind. For night attacks, fire can be set windward while the attack can be carried out from the opposite direction. Your allies should be mindful of this also. One should always hang wind-bells in order to know the direction of the wind.

Lord Aki declared that he would not have his descendants learn military tactics. He said, "On the battlefield, once discretion starts it cannot be stopped. One will not break through to the enemy with discretion. Indiscretion is most important when in front of the tiger's den. Therefore, if one were informed of military tactics, he would have many doubts, and there will be no end to the matter. My descendants will not practice military tactics.'

According to Lord Naoshige's words:

There is something to which every young samurai should pay attention. During times of peace when listening to stories of battle, one should never say, "In facing such a situation, what would a person do?" Such words are out of the question. How will a man who has doubts even in his own room achieve anything on the battlefield? There is a saying that goes, "No matter what the circumstances might be, one should be of the mind to win. One should be holding the first spear to strike." Even though you have put your life on the line, there is nothing to be done when the situation doesn't go as planned.

Takeda Shingen once said, "If there was a man who could kill Lord Ieyasu, I would give him a handsome reward." Hearing this, a boy of thirteen entered into the service of Lord Ieyasu and one night when he saw that Ieyasu had retired, took a stab at his bedding. Lord Ieyasu was actually in the next room silently reading a sutra, but he quickly grabbed the boy.

When the investigation was held, the boy related the facts honestly, and Lord Ieyasu said, "You seemed to be an excellent young man, so I employed you on friendly terms. Now, however, I am even more impressed by you." He then sent the lad back to Shingen.

One night some samurai from Karatsu gathered together and were playing go. Master Kitabatake was watching the game, and when he offered a suggestion, one man attacked him with a sword. After the people around them had stopped the man, Master Kitabatake pinched out the light of the candle and said, "It was nothing more than my own indiscretion, and I apologize. The sword hit the go case; I was not the least bit wounded."

Then the candle was relighted, but when the man came to reconciliate and offer him a sake cup, Kitabatake cut the man's head off with one blow. Presently he said, "My thigh having been cut through, it was difficult to offer any resistance, but by binding my leg with my coat and supporting myself with the go board, I have done this thing." Having said this, he expired.

There is nothing so painful as regret. We would all like to be without it. However, when we are very happy and become elated, or when we habitually jump into something thoughtlessly, later we are distraught, and it is for the most part because we did not think ahead and are now regretful. Certainly we should try not to become dejected, and when very happy should calm our minds.

These are teachings of Yamamoto Jin'emon:

- Singlemindedness is all-powerful.
- Tether even a roasted chicken.
- Continue to spur a running horse.
- A man who will criticize you openly carries no connivance.
- A man exists for a generation, but his name lasts to the end of time.
- Money is a thing that will be there when asked for. A good man is not so easily found.
- Walk with a real man one hundred yards and he'll tell you at least seven lies.
- To ask when you already know is politeness. To ask when you don't know is the rule.
- Wrap your intentions in needles of pine.
- One should not open his mouth wide or yawn in front of another. Do this behind your fan or sleeve.
- A straw hat or helmet should be worn tilled toward the front.

It is a principle of the art of war that one should simply lay down his life and strike. If one's opponent also does the same, it is an even match. Defeating one's opponent is then a matter of faith and destiny.

One should not show his sleeping quarters to other people. The times of deep sleep and dawning are very important. One should be mindful of this. This is from a story by Nagahama Inosuke.

When one departs for the front, he should carry rice in a bag. His underwear should be made from the skin of a badger. This way he will not have lice. In a long campaign, lice are troublesome.

When meeting with the enemy, there is a way to determine his strength. If he has his head cast down, he will appear black and is strong. If he is looking upward, he will appear white and is weak. This is from a story by Natsume Toneri.

If a warrior is not unattached to life and death, he will be of no use whatsoever. The saying that "All abilities come from one mind" sounds as though it has to do with sentient matters, but it is in fact a matter of being unattached to life and death. With such non-attachment one can accomplish any feat. Martial arts and the like are related to this insofar as they can lead to the Way.

To calm one's mind, one swallows his saliva. This is a secret matter. When one becomes angry, it is the same. Putting spittle on one's forehead is also good. In the Yoshida school of archery, swallowing one's spittle is the secret principle of the art.

A certain general said, "For soldiers other than officers, if they would test their armor, they should test only the front. Furthermore, while ornamentation on armor is unnecessary, one should be very careful about the appearance of his helmet. It is something that accompanies his head to the enemy's camp."

Nakano Jin'emon said, "Learning such things as military tactics is useless. If one does not strike out by simply closing his eyes and rushing into the enemy, even if it is only one step, he will be of no use." This was also the opinion of Iyanaga Sasuke.

In Natsume Toneri's "Military Stories" it is written: "Look at the soldiers of recent times! Even in long battles there are hardly one or two occasions when blood is washed with blood. One should not be negligent." Toneri was a ronin from the Kamigata area.

To have execution grounds in a place where travelers come and go is useless. The executions in Edo and the Kamigala area are meant to be an example for the whole country. But the executions in one province are only for an example in that province. If crimes are many, it is a province's shame. How would this look to other provinces?

With the passing of time, the criminal will forget the reason for his crime; it is best to execute him on the spot.

Matsudaira Izu no kami said to Master Mizuno Kenmotsu, "You're such a useful person, it's a shame that you're so short."

Kenmotsu replied, "That's true. Sometimes things in this world don't go the way we would like. Now if I were to cut off your head and attach it to the bottom of my feet, I would be taller. But that's something that couldn't be done."

A certain person was passing by the town of Yae when suddenly his stomach began to hurt. He stopped at a house on a side street and asked to use the toilet. There was only a young woman there, but she took him to the back and showed him where it was. Just as he was taking off his hakama and going into the toilet, the woman's husband came home and accused them both of adultery. In the end, it became a public matter.

Lord Naoshige heard the case and said, "Even if this is not a matter of adultery, it is the same as adultery to take off one's hakama without hesitation in a place where there is an unaccompanied woman, and in the woman's case to allow someone to disrobe while her husband is absent from home."

It is said that they were both condemned to death for this act.

In assessing the enemy's castle there is a saying that goes, "Smoke and mist are like looking at a spring mountain. After the rain is like viewing a clear day." There is weakness in perfect clarity.

Among the words spoken by great generals, there are some that were said offhandedly. One should not receive these words in the same manner, however.

People who have an intelligent appearance will not be outstanding even if they do something good, and if they do something normal, people will think them lacking. But if a person who is thought of as having a gentle disposition does even a slightly good thing, he will be praised by people.

On the fourteenth day of the seventh month in the third year of Shotoku, there were some cooks in the midst of preparations for the Ben Festival in the outer citadel of the castle. One of them, Hara Jurozaemon, unsheathed his sword and cut off the head of Sagara Genzaemon. Mawatari Rokuuemon, Aiura Tarobei, Kola Kinbei and Kakihara Riemen all ran away in confusion. When Jurozaemon sighted Kinbei and started chasing him, the latter fled to the foot soldiers' gathering area. There, the daimyo's palanquin attendant, Tanaka Takeuemon, stood against Jurozaemon and took away his still drawn sword. Ishirnaru San'emon chased Jurozaemon, and when they came to the foot soldiers' area, assisted Takeuemon.

The punishment was given on the twenty-ninth day of the eleventh month in the same year. Jurozaemon was bound with rope and beheaded. Rokuuemon, Tarobei, Kinbei and Riemon were banished, and San'emon was ordered to retire. Takeuemon was rewarded with three pieces of silver.

It was later said that Takeuemon had been slow to act, for he had not bound the man at that time.

Among Takeda Shingen's retainers there were men of matchless courage, but when Katsuyori was killed in the fight at Tenmokuzan, they all fled. Tsuchiya Sozo, a warrior who had been in disfavor for many years, came out alone, however, and said, "I wonder where all the men are who spoke so bravely every day? I shall return the master's favors to me." And he fell alone in battle.

The essentials of speaking are in not speaking at all. If you think that you can finish something without speaking, finish it without saying a single word. If there is something that cannot be accomplished without speaking, one should speak with few words, in a way that will accord well with reason.

To open one's mouth indiscriminately brings shame, and there are many times when people will turn their backs on such a person.

A devotee of the Nembutsu recites the Buddha's name with every incoming and outgoing breath in order never to forget the Buddha. A retainer, too, should be just like this in thinking of his master. Not to forget one's master is the most fundamental thing for a retainer.

Men who did well at the time of their death were men of real bravery. There are many examples of such. But people who talk in an accomplished fashion every day yet are agitated at the time of their death can be known not to have true bravery.

In the secret principles of Yagyu Tajima no kami Munenori there is the saying, "There are no military tactics for a man of great strength." As proof of this, there was once a certain vassal of the shogun who came to Master Yagyu and asked to become a disciple. Master Yagyu said, "You seem to be a man who is very accomplished in some school of martial art. Let us make the master disciple contract after I learn the name of the school."

But the man replied, "I have never practiced one of the martial arts."

Master Yagyu said, "Have you come to make sport of Tajima no kami? Is my perception amiss in thinking that you are a teacher to the shogun?" But the man swore to it and Master Yagyu then asked, "That being so, do you not have some deep conviction?"

The man replied, "When I was a child, I once became suddenly aware that a warrior is a man who does not hold his life in regret. Since I have held that in my heart for many years, it has become a deep conviction, and today I never think about death. Other than that I have no special conviction."

Master Yagyu was deeply impressed and said, "My perceptions were not the least bit awry. The deepest principle of my military tactics is just that one thing. Lip until now, among all the many hundreds of disciples I have had, there is not one who is licensed in this deepest principle. It is not necessary for you to take up the wooden sword. I will initiate you right now." And it is said that he promptly banded him the certified scroll. This is a story of Muragawa Soden's.

Meditation on inevitable death should be performed daily. Every day when one's body and mind are at peace, one should meditate upon being ripped apart by arrows, rifles, spears and swords, being carried away by surging waves, being thrown into the midst of a great fire, being struck by lightning, being shaken to death by a great earthquake, falling from thousand-foot cliffs, dying of disease or committing seppuku at the death of one's master. And every day without fail one should consider himself as dead.

There is a saying of the elders' that goes, "Step from under the eaves and you're a dead man. Leave the gate and the enemy is waiting." This is not a matter of being careful. It is to consider oneself as dead beforehand.

People will become your enemies if you become eminent too quickly in life, and you will be ineffectual. Rising slowly in the world, people will be your allies and your happiness will he assured. In the long run, whether you are fast or slow, as long as you have people's understanding there will be no danger. It is said that fortune that is urged upon you from others is the most effective.

The warriors of old cultivated mustaches, for as proof that a man had been slain in battle, his ears and nose would be cut off and brought to the enemy's camp. So that there would be no mistake as to whether the person was a man or a woman, the mustache was also cut off with the nose. At such a time the head was thrown away if it had no mustache, for it might be mistaken for that of a woman. Therefore, growing a mustache was one of the disciplines of a samurai so that his head would not be thrown away upon his death. Tsunetomo said, "If one washes his face with water every morning, if he is slain his complexion will not change."

The word "person of the north" comes from a tradition of the correct way of upbringing. A couple will put their pillows in the west, and the man, lying on the south side, will face the north, while the woman, lying on the north side, will face the south.

In bringing up a boy, one should first encourage a sense of valor. From the time he is young the child should liken his parents to the master, and learn everyday politeness and etiquette, the serving of other people, the ways of speech, forbearance and even the correct way of walking down the street. The elders were taught in the same fashion. When he does not put effort into things, he should be scolded and made to go the entire day without eating. This is also one of the disciplines of a retainer.

As for a girl, it is most important to teach her chastity from the time she is a child. She should not be in the company of a man at a distance of less than six feet, nor should she meet them eye to eye, nor should she receive things from them directly from hand to hand. Neither should she go sightseeing or take trips to temples. A woman who has been brought up strictly and has endured suffering at her own borne will suffer no ennui after she is married.

In dealing with younger children one should use rewards and punishments. If one is lax in being sure that they do as they are told, young children will become self-interested and will later be involved in wrongdoings. It is something about which one should be very careful.

CHAPTER 12

Late night idle talk

AS A RETAINER of the Nabeshima clan, one should have the intention of studying our province's history and traditions, but provincial studies are made light of nowadays. The basic reason for this study is to understand the foundation of our clan, and to know that the clan's forefathers established its perpetuity by means of their suffering and compassion. The fact that our clan has perpetually continued in an unrivaled manner up to this very day is due to the humanity and martial valor of Master Ryuzoji Iekane, the charity and faith of Master Nabeshima Kiyohisa, and the appearance of Lord Ryuzoji Takanobu and Lord Nabeshima Naoshige and their might.

I am at a complete loss when it comes to understanding why people of this generation have forgotten these things and respect the Buddhas of other places. Neither the Shakyamuni Buddha, nor Confucius, nor Kusunoki, nor Shingen were ever retainers of the Ryuzojis or the Nabeshimas; hence it cannot be said that they are in harmony with our clan's customs. In times of war or in times of peace it would be sufficient if both the upper and lower classes would worship our ancestors and study their teachings. One worships the head of whatever clan or discipline to which he belongs. Outside learning for retainers of our clan is worthless. One may think that it is fine to study other disciplines as a diversion after his provincial studies are replete. Yet if a person has a good understanding of provincial studies, he will see that there is nothing lacking in them.

Today, if someone from another clan were to ask about the origin of the Ryuzojis and the Nabeshimas, or why the fief was transferred from the former to the latter, or if they were to ask something like, "I have heard that the Ryuzojis and the Nabeshimas are the greatest in Kyushu for deeds of martial valor, but can you tell me some of the particulars?" I suppose that the man with no knowledge of provincial studies would not be able to answer a word.

For a retainer there should be nothing other than doing his own job. For the most part people dislike their own jobs, find those of others more interesting, cause misunderstanding, and bring on utter disasters. Good models of men who performed their duty in their work are Lord Naoshige and Lord Katsushige. The retainers of those times all performed their duties. From the upper classes, men who would be of good use were searched out, while from the lower classes men desired to be useful. The minds of the two classes were of mutual accord, and the strength of the clan was secure.

In all our generations of masters there has never been a bad or foolish one, and in the end there has never been one who ranked second or third among the daimyo of Japan. It is truly a wonderful clan; this is due to the faith of its founders. Moreover, they did not send the clan's retainers to other provinces. nor did they invite men from other provinces in. Men who were made ronin were kept within the province, as were the descendants of those who were made to commit seppuku. The wonder of being born into a clan with such a deep pledge between master and servant is an inexpressible blessing, passed down through the apes, for both farmer and townsman. This goes without saying for the retainer.

The foundation of a Nabeshima samurai should be in knowing this fact; in being deeply resolved to return this blessing by being useful; in serving more and more selflessly when treated kindly by the master; in knowing that being made a ronin or being ordered to commit seppuku are also forms of service; and in aiming to be mindful of the clan forever, whether one is banished deep in the mountains or buried under the earth. Although it is unfitting for someone like me to say this, in dying it is my hope not to become a Buddha. Rather, my will is permeated with the resolution to help manage the affairs of the province, though I be reborn as a Nabeshima samurai seven times. One needs neither vitality nor talent. In a word, it is a matter of having the will to shoulder the clan by oneself.

How can one human being be inferior to another? In all matters of discipline, one will be useless unless he has great pride. Unless one is determined to move the clan by himself, all his discipline will come to naught. Although, like a tea kettle, it is easy for one's enthusiasm to cool, there is a way to keep this from happening. My own vows are the following:

Never to be outdone in the Way of the Samurai.

To be of good use to the master.

To be filial to my parents.

- To manifest great compassion, and to act for the sake of Man.

If one dedicates these four vows to the gods and Buddhas every morning, he will have the strength of two men and will never slip backward. One must edge forward like the inchworm, bit by bit. The gods and Buddhas, too, first started with a vow.

Made in the USA
Monee, IL
12 April 2020